Beach Life

Rehoboth Beach Reads

Short Stories by Local Writers

Edited by Nancy Sakaduski

Cat & Mouse Press
Lewes, DE 19958
www.catandmousepress.com

Published 2017.ISBN: 978-0-9968052-7-8

PERMISSION AND ACKNOWLEDGMENTS

Cover illustration/book design by Emory Au. © 2017 Emory Au.

Copy editing by Joyce Mochrie, One Last Look.

REPRINTED WITH PERMISSION:

"A Beautifully Disturbing Day at the Beach," John Edmonds. © 2017 John M. Edmonds.

"A Day in the Life," David Strauss. © 2017 David Strauss.

"And the Sea Hath Spoken," Darryl Forrest. © 2017 Darryl C. Forrest, Jr.

"Bottleneck at Hole 14," Renay Regardie. © 2017 Renay Regardie.

"Hole in One," Amanda Linehan. © 2017 Amanda Linehan.

"Lefty and the Empty Bucket of Fries," Tony Houck. © 2017 Anthony E. Houck.

"Life Starts on Tiptoes," Lonn Braender. © 2017 Lonn Braender.

"Not in My World," Kathleen Martens. © 2017 Kathleen L. Martens.

"Ralphie to the Rescue," Carl Schiessl. © 2017 Carl J. Schiessl.

"Rearrangements," Marie Lathers. © 2017 Marie Lathers.

"Secrets," Amber Tamosaitis. © 2017 Amber Tamosaitis.

"Some Girls," Michael Sprouse. © 2017 Michael Sprouse.

"The Bench," Jenny Scott. © 2017 Jennifer Scott.

"The Bomber Jacket," Jackson Coppley. © 2017 Jackson Coppley.

"The Boy on the Bike," Susan Miller. © 2017 Suzanne M. Miller.

"The Fog," Linda Chambers. © 2017 Linda Huntly Chambers.

"The Mime's Niece," Emily Zasada. © 2017 Emily Zasada.

"The Nereid's Wedding," Elizabeth Michaelson Monaghan.
© 2017 Elizabeth Michaelson Monaghan.

"The Shot Shared Round the World," Joy Givens. © 2017 Joy Givens.

"The Stranger and the Horseshoe," Alex Hannah. © 2017 Alexander H. Hannah.

"The Sweet Truth," Jeanie P. Blair. © 2017 Jean Pitrizzi Blair.

"The Swimsuit Issue," Chris Jacobsen. © 2017 Christiana D. Jacobsen.

"The Understudy," Terri Kiral. © 2017 Theresa Kuenzer.

"Too Many Hemingways," Joseph L. Crossen. © 2017 Joseph L. Crossen.

"We Found Buried Pirate Treasure!," Douglas Harrell. © 2017 Douglas Gaines Harrell.

Table of Contents

Hole in One, *Amanda Linehan*..*1*

The Mime's Niece, *Emily Zasada*..*9*

The Fog, *Linda Chambers*...*21*

Too Many Hemingways, *Joseph L. Crossen*.....................................*27*

Not in My World, *Kathleen Martens*...*37*

The Bomber Jacket, *Jackson Coppley*..*49*

Ralphie to the Rescue, *Carl Schiessl*...*53*

The Swimsuit Issue, *Chris Jacobsen*..*65*

A Beautifully Disturbing Day at the Beach, *John Edmonds*................*75*

Rearrangements, *Marie Lathers*..*83*

Some Girls, *Michael Sprouse*...*89*

The Nereid's Wedding, *Elizabeth Michaelson Monaghan*.................*101*

Life Starts on Tiptoes, *Lonn Braender*...*113*

Secrets, *Amber Tamosaitis*..*123*

The Boy on the Bike, *Susan Miller*..*133*

The Stranger and the Horseshoe, *Alex Hannah*..............................*139*

The Bench, *Jenny Scott*..*143*

We Found Buried Pirate Treasure!, *Douglas Harrell*........................*147*

The Sweet Truth, *Jeanie P. Blair*...*155*

A Day in the Life, *David Strauss*..*169*

And the Sea Hath Spoken, *Darryl Forrest*.....................................*177*

Lefty and the Empty Bucket of Fries, *Tony Houck*.........................*189*

Bottleneck at Hole 14, *RenayRegardie*..*201*

The Shot Shared Round the World, *Joy Givens*..............................*211*

The Understudy, *Terri Kiral*...*225*

PREFACE

These are the winning stories from the 2017 Rehoboth Beach Reads Short Story Contest, sponsored by Browseabout Books. Writers were asked to create a story—fiction or nonfiction—that fit the theme "Beach Life" and had a connection to Rehoboth Beach. A panel of judges chose the stories they thought were best and those selections have been printed here for your enjoyment. Like *The Beach House*, *The Boardwalk*, *Beach Days*, and *Beach Nights* (other books in this series), this book contains more than just "they went down to the beach and had a picnic" stories. The quality and diversity of the stories is simply amazing.

For contact information or other Cat & Mouse Press publications, go to: www.catandmousepress.com.

ACKNOWLEDGEMENTS

Thanks to Browseabout Books for their continued outstanding support. We are so lucky to have this great store in the heart of our community. They have supported the Rehoboth Beach Reads Short Story Contest from day one and continue to be the go-to place for books, gifts, and other fun stuff.

I thank both the Rehoboth Beach Writers' Guild and the Eastern Shore Writers Association for their support and service to the writing community. These two organizations provide an amazing array of educational programming, and many of the writers whose stories appear in this book benefitted from their classes, meetings, and events.

I thank this year's judges, Stephanie Fowler, Barbara Lockhart, Laurel Marshfield, Mary Pauer, William Peak, and Judith Reveal, who gave generously of their valuable time.

Special thanks to Emory Au, who captured the theme so well in the cover illustration and who designed and laid out the interior of this book as well.

I also thank Cindy Myers, queen of the mermaids, for her continued loyalty and support.

An extra-special thank-you to my husband, Joe, who helps on many levels and puts up with a great deal.

I would also like to thank the writers—those whose work is in this book and those whose work was not chosen. Putting a piece of writing up for judging takes courage. Thank you for being brave. Keep writing and submitting your work!

—*Nancy Sakaduski*

Hole in One

By Amanda Linehan

The wind blew at my face, carrying with it the smell of boardwalk fries, which I had come to associate with the beach as much as the rhythm of the ocean and the feel of hot sand on my feet.

As a kid, I had not been to the beach much—only once or twice—and it was only when I started dating Jason, who is now my fiancé, that I visited on any kind of a regular basis. He gripped my hand as we walked next to each other on the boardwalk, having decided to take a break from baking on the beach.

"Hey, Carolyn," Jason said, tugging me over to an arcade entrance. "Want me to win you a huge teddy bear?"

"No," I promptly replied, with scarcely a smile on my face. But Jason laughed like one of the kids playing Skee-Ball inside.

"Yeah, I didn't think so," he said, still smiling, knowing full well that huge teddy bears weren't my thing.

Beach culture was still interesting to me. What Jason took for granted after three decades of summers at the beach, I still found intriguing, if odd. The mini-golf, the T-shirts with crude sayings, the fact that flip-flops were welcome anywhere, under any conditions (Jason wanted us both to wear them at our wedding), and, of course, the boardwalk fries, which were practically a religion unto themselves.

Jason smiled his big, goofy smile, probably still thinking about the huge teddy bear that he really did want to win for me, and I realized that one day I should let him.

I had never played a game of mini-golf, although Jason begged me every time we came down to his family's beach house. I just couldn't understand the appeal. I didn't want to play regular golf, and I surely didn't want to do it with a large windmill spinning in my way.

"Hey, let's get some fries," Jason said, and started pulling me in the direction of Thrasher's. I acquiesced gladly. Unlike huge teddy bears, boardwalk fries were definitely my thing.

Weaving through the crowd gathered in front of Ryan's Mini Golf, Jason pulled me along urgently. He was a little ahead of me, and in his rush to purchase a bucket of fries, he pulled me into a girl of about ten. She staggered a little, then fell over, breaking her fall with two nimble hands, after which she looked up at me. I dropped Jason's hand and offered her my own.

"I'm so sorry," I said, as I saw Jason look back and call out "Carolyn?" in a confused and mildly distressed manner. I helped the girl up from the ground, and she wiped her hands off on a little pair of blue shorts.

"It's okay," she said, and I hoped she wasn't going to start crying. "I was just looking for someone to play mini-golf with."

Jason had caught back up with me and looked at the girl. "Hey, sorry about that. Are you okay?"

"Yeah, I'm okay."

"You sure?"

"Yeah. It's just that I really wanted to play mini-golf, and my grandma says she's too old to play." The girl waved at an elderly woman who sat across the boardwalk on a bench. The woman smiled warmly and waved back.

I smiled back at the little girl's grandmother. "Don't you have any other family members who can play with you?"

"No. It's just my grandma and me."

I exchanged a look with Jason.

"Well, if it's okay with your grandma, maybe we'll play a game with you."

"It's okay! It's okay!" the girl said, jumping up and down. "She gave me five bucks to play."

Jason turned to me. "Your first mini-golf!" He pumped a fist in the air.

"What's your name?" I asked the girl.

"Daisy," the girl replied.

"Well, I'm Carolyn and this is Jason. I've never played mini-golf before."

"Really?" Daisy said, squinting her eyes up at me.

"Really," I said, and the three of us walked past the sign that said "Ryan's Mini Golf" and up the stairs.

As we neared the top, Jason whispered to me, "Why don't we just pick this up?"

I looked at him and nodded back. He paid for the three of us, and we got our clubs and golf balls. Jason teased Daisy about something and I heard the two of them laughing, while I admired the view and got another whiff of boardwalk fries. When I turned around, Jason was still laughing, and I had a split-second view of the future right before my eyes.

"All right, so where do we start?" I asked.

Daisy skipped to the hole marked "1" and announced that she would go first. Jason and I exchanged smiles and glances.

Daisy placed her ball down carefully and moved to its left. She stood very still, concentrated for a few seconds, and then swung her club.

The ball rolled up a hill and down. When it stopped moving, it was just a few inches from the hole. An easy putt. (Even I knew that.)

"Yay!" Daisy said, jumping up and down. "I almost got it in the hole!"

I couldn't help but smile at Jason. Maybe mini-golf would be fun after all.

Daisy finished taking her turn, and Jason wrote down a "2" by her name on the scorecard. It was my turn. And let's just say I did a little worse than Daisy.

I couldn't control the path of the ball at all, what with the little hills and curves. I'd try to hit it toward a certain spot, and it would end up going the opposite way. I'd hit the ball too lightly on a hill, so it didn't make it over the top and rolled back down. Or I'd hit it too hard and the ball would fly around the little green, more like pinball than golf. When all was said and done, Jason wrote down a "9" for me on the scorecard. He took his turn and scored a four. Then it started all over again.

At each hole, Daisy would go through her routine. Place the ball down, take a moment of quiet, and swing. I realized that she must have played a lot this summer—and maybe past summers, too—because she seemed to know every hole on the course.

Jason took a moment to tally the scores halfway through and, no surprise, Daisy was winning, Jason was in second, and I was a distant third. But I was having fun.

"Hey! I've got an idea," Daisy called out, swinging her club by her side in the careless, reckless manner of children. "If I win, we have to play again."

"And what will we get if one of us wins?" Jason asked with a grin.

Daisy wrinkled her forehead and said earnestly, "I don't know."

Jason and I both laughed.

"Hadn't thought that far ahead, huh?" Jason put a friendly hand on Daisy's shoulder. "Well, what do you think, Carolyn?"

I was thinking about boardwalk fries. Even though this had turned out better than I expected, I didn't think I was in the mood for another game.

"Uhhhh," I started, and Jason picked up on my answer.

"Tell you what," Jason said, "we can't play another game with you, but if you win, we'll pay for your next game and maybe someone else will play with you."

"Another game! Yay!" Daisy jumped up and down. She stepped up to the next hole and got ready to swing. After a moment's concentration, she hit the ball and it sailed toward the hole. It was like watching it in slow motion. Up one hill, down the next, curve to the right, slow down just enough, and bang—a hole in one.

"Wow!" I said, voicing my surprise out loud.

Jason let out a low whistle. "Nice one!"

Daisy picked her ball out of the hole. "My first hole in one this summer!"

Jason high-fived her as I stepped up to take my turn. I scored a three, my best score yet. As I high-fived Jason, I thought that maybe this was an easier hole to play—considering my score and Daisy's hole in one—but Jason ended up getting a six, his worst score, so maybe not.

"Hey," Jason called out after we had all taken turns and were standing by the next hole, "I'll throw in a bucket of fries to our little deal if you get a hole in one on this one, too. But," Jason held up a finger, "if you don't, then the deal is off. No extra game. What do you say?"

"You mean the $10 bucket?"

"Yep."

"Okay," Daisy said, and stepped up to the next hole.

Another hole in one.

She jumped around and Jason laughed.

At the next hole, she scored a two, to which she replied, "dang it!" while I continued to struggle as we made our way around the course.

There were three holes left, and I was now feeling ready to leave my first mini-golf experience behind and commence with the boardwalk fries eating, but Jason still seemed eager.

"All right, Daisy, besides French fries and mini-golf, what else is your favorite thing on the boardwalk?" Jason asked. I tried to catch his attention to no avail.

"Arcades," Daisy said, swinging her club around haphazardly again.

"Okay, so if you get a hole in one on this hole, I'll throw in another

$10 to go play in the arcade. No strings attached. But it has to be this hole, this turn, okay?"

"Okay!" Daisy said and jumped up and down before regaining her composure at the start of the hole.

"Jason," I whispered loudly, getting close to him. "I don't think this is a good idea."

He waved me off and whispered back, "It's fine. She was just lucky. She'll never get this one."

I tilted my head and gave him a look, and he mouthed back at me "it's fine."

Jason looked genuinely shocked, and his smile wavered as Daisy's ball rolled into the hole. He opened his wallet. I couldn't believe he was about to give this girl twenty-five dollars. "A deal's a deal," he said, his brow just a little wrinkled as Daisy held out her hand to receive the bills.

"Thanks," she said, stuffing the money into her shorts pocket. "This was really fun."

We headed back down the stairs and I couldn't wait to return Daisy to her grandma, though Jason still seemed to be upbeat, chatting and laughing with Daisy on the way down.

Back on the boardwalk, it was still crowded and we re-entered the throng.

"Hey, let's go tell your grandma what a great mini-golf player you are," Jason said.

Daisy looked up the boardwalk once, and then again, as if she were looking for someone, though I could see her grandma still sitting on the bench across from us.

"Okay," she said, and took a glance in the opposite direction.

Ready to get on my way, I strode over to the old woman on the bench, Jason right beside me. "Hi," I said, as I got within earshot, "your granddaughter is quite the mini-golf player."

The old woman smiled at me warmly, then scrunched up her eyes and tilted her head.

"Granddaughter?" she said.

"Yes." I turned around looking for Daisy, though the crowd was so thick I couldn't immediately pinpoint her. "Daisy. She asked us to play mini-golf with her. Gave me my first game, actually."

Recognition dawned on the old woman's face as she said, "Oh, you mean the little girl in the blue shorts who's been waving at me all morning. She's not my granddaughter, but she was so darling, I just couldn't help but wave back. Now what's this about mini-golf?"

Stunned, I looked all around for Daisy, but all I saw was Jason pointing and a little blue-shorted girl running down the boardwalk in her flip-flops, thirty feet away and gaining ground.

Jason made a sheepish grin. "Oh, well."

I shook my head as a seagull squawked right above us. I swear it sounded just like, "suckers!"

AMANDA LINEHAN IS A FICTION WRITER, INDIE AUTHOR, AND INFP (ONE OF MYERS-BRIGGS PERSONALITY TYPES). SHE HAS PUBLISHED FOUR NOVELS AND A COUPLE OF HANDFULS OF SHORT STORIES. HER SHORT FICTION HAS BEEN FEATURED IN *EVERY DAY FICTION*. SHE LIVES IN MARYLAND, LIKES TO BE OUTSIDE, AND WRITES WITH HER CAT SLEEPING ON THE FLOOR BESIDE HER DESK. CHECK OUT MORE OF AMANDA'S FICTION AT HER WEBSITE: WWW.AMANDALINEHAN.COM

The Mime's Niece

By Emily Zasada

Molly didn't want to be at the bank—didn't want to, in fact, leave Rehoboth at all—but she was tired of all the notices from the power company threatening that the power was about to be cut off, not to mention the equally threatening notices from the water and gas utilities, so there she was. In the forty-five minutes she'd been there, the woman behind the desk had already attempted to upsell her on some sort of CD, a special premiere checking account, and designer checks.

Outside the window, a homeless man sipped something out of a paper bag and spat onto the parking lot. It was one o'clock in the afternoon. Over the strip mall, the sky was the flat, endless blue that heralded the start of summer. Carl had loved summer; that was when what he thought of as his real life began. Molly couldn't stand the thought that this was the first year he wouldn't be around for any of it.

Inside the bank, everything was gray and perfectly clean. On a central counter, deposit slips were arranged in optimistic stacks.

"I'll just be a few more minutes," the woman said, tapping on her keyboard. She was wearing a gray suit and matching gray eyeshadow. "Would you like any tea or coffee or—"

"No, nothing." Molly watched a man on his way into the store stop in the middle of the parking lot, pull a stack of coupons out of his pocket, and start flipping through them. He was wearing a flannel shirt, even though it was eighty degrees, and the buttons weren't lined up quite right. A seagull landed on a light pole over his head, screeching wildly. Molly decided to try being friendly. *That's what Carl would have done*, she thought. "At least you get to see people.

The last time I worked in an office, I only saw the mirrored windows in the office building next to mine. If I tried very hard, by going over to the window and craning my neck, I could see little people down below, crossing the street—"

The woman briefly paused her typing. "Is that so," the woman said. An unconvincing imitation of a smile flashed on her face and then died as she frowned at something on her screen. "I just have a few last questions before I print out your paperwork and we're done. What is your occupation?"

Molly swallowed. There it was—the problem from which she could never escape. It had even followed her here, to this lonely and terrible strip mall. She thought of Uncle Carl's videos on YouTube, and how she'd been playing them over and over, and practicing, albeit badly, standing in Uncle Carl's living room and looking out at the waves crashing onto the beach, trying to imagine a rope with a great weight attached to it in her hands. Pulling on it.

"Mime," Molly said. "Put down 'mime.' "

* * * * *

When Molly got home, Joe was sitting on the front step. She hadn't seen him in more than six months, but she wasn't all that surprised. She hadn't been checking the messages on Carl's phone or her own, but she'd suspected most of the recent phone calls had been from him. There was an anxious quality to the way the phone had been ringing that she associated with Joe.

"My wife kicked me out," he said, not looking at Molly. "I told her everything. You haven't been answering your phone."

Molly sighed and walked up the steps to unlock the door. The wind from the ocean was fierce. She'd known Joe would be back. Technically, she could tell him to leave if she wanted to, but she could never do that to Carl. Even if Carl was dead.

"After you," she said. "You know about the extra key under the rabbit? Just use that for now. And I think you still have the key to the workshop?"

"Yes." He hesitated. "Thank you."

Molly wanted to say that it was what Carl would have wanted, but she didn't know if she could say his name out loud without tearing up, and she didn't want to do that in front of Joe. "Sure," she said.

* * * * *

That afternoon, Molly went to pay as many of the utilities as she could in person with the new starter checks she'd gotten from the bank. It wasn't fun, but she was tired of lying awake at night, waiting and worrying about the inevitable moment that the air conditioner and the ceiling fan would grind to a halt. Besides, it was her one afternoon off from the souvenir shop. She was going to be tied up for the rest of the week, putting away the new shipments of crab magnets and crab-shaped bottle openers that heralded the start of the season. The hermit crabs were on their way, too; she'd checked the tracking number just that morning. Those were her favorite. She liked to let them walk up and down her arms when no one was in the store.

On her way back, Molly stopped at her favorite Chinese food place but hesitated at the counter as she was placing her order. When Carl was alive, she'd had dinner with both of them together, but never just dinner with Joe alone. She wasn't sure if she should pick anything up for him, but thought if she didn't, it would be rude. Not to mention that there were all those commas and digits in Carl's bank account balance. She could certainly afford it now.

"Two orders of vegetable lo mein, please."

* * * * *

Molly set the table on the back deck, and Joe brought out the food containers. Joe was grimy from working in the workshop all afternoon, but he didn't seem to be aware of it, and Molly didn't care. They ate mostly in silence, the ocean so loud it made talking difficult anyway. *No better soundtrack*, Uncle Carl always said.

After dinner, Joe put the trash in a plastic bag and Molly gathered up the recycling.

On his way out the door, Joe asked, "So how's it going, anyway? With your divorce, I mean."

"Oh—" Molly was caught off guard. He'd made it sound like such a chummy question, as if he'd been asking what she thought about the Orioles' early season performance. Not to mention that she and Joe had never talked about anything personal, unless Carl had been in the room as a sort of buffer between them. She wasn't sure if she wanted him to start becoming friendly toward her. It would be uncharted territory. "You know. A holding pattern. In Maryland, you have to be separated for a year. I don't know about Virginia—"

"A year, since we have kids." Joe sighed. "You're lucky that there aren't kids in your situation."

Molly didn't know what to say to that. She couldn't imagine having children. She wasn't sure how good she was at looking after herself, even.

"I'm going to sweep the deck before the seagulls move in," she said, and grabbed the broom.

* * * * *

A few days later, on the large, flat-screen television in the living room, she was playing one of the dozens of YouTube videos of Uncle Carl uploaded by tourists over the last several years, imitating him as he went through the glass wall routine, placing her hands flat in front of her on an imaginary, vertical plane in space. Outside, she could hear the rattling hum of Joe's arc welder, which comforted her for some reason. She was playing the video so it looped over and over. The only sound in the video was of the ocean in the background and of a child asking again and again why he couldn't see the wall. Carl's face, even under the face paint he wore, was so familiar that Molly couldn't look at it without feeling a forlorn ping.

Once, during the video, he glanced directly at the camera. Every time the video looped back to that point, Molly liked to imagine that he was alive and back in his living room with her, telling her to watch. *Make sure it always feels new to you, whatever it is that you're doing. If it feels like routine to you, it will feel routine to them, and they'll wander away, looking for the funnel cakes or French fries or whatever it was they were looking for when they found you.*

She was concentrating so hard that she didn't hear the sliding glass door open, and didn't know that Joe was behind her until she heard his voice. "You're not very good at that," he said.

She was trying to think of some snappy retort when she saw the tears in his eyes and realized that he was staring at the video of Carl. On the screen, Carl was opening an imaginary doorknob and smiling at the crowd.

"Sorry," Molly said, fumbling for the remote.

"It's your house," Joe said, on his way out of the room.

* * * * *

Once, Molly was just like everyone else, or at least she did a better job at pretending. She was married to a man she met at a friend's wedding, someone with pleasant features and admirable goals who also looked good in a jacket. When they met, they were relieved, both thinking that finding someone who wanted to stay with them was all they needed to do. Now, they could relax and continue with their lives, which had become more complicated than either could have guessed, before they became full-fledged adults.

They bought a condo together in Annapolis, which Molly did her best to like, even though it was small and stared out on a stark rectangle of the parking lot. At night, a streetlamp blazed so close to their bedroom window that Molly would sometimes wake up confused about whether it was night or day.

Molly had a series of jobs, mostly in marketing or administration—or both. She hated all of them. She would sit in meetings and stare at everyone's faces, wondering if anyone really meant anything they were saying.

One day in May, she was at her desk, the weak light filtering through the grayish glass in the office windows. She was waiting for an email from a friend whom she suspected wasn't too great of a friend, but she was hoping to hear from her anyway because it would at least be a distraction. She kept switching back and forth from her email program to the task she was working on, some endless project management tool with little squares she had to click to fill in. She looked down the row of cubicles and saw everyone else immersed in the same thing.

She thought about how small their movements were. How small everything was. The empty conversations in the conference rooms about obscure, inconsequential things. The flickering of her coworkers' eyes as people walked by their cubicles.

Through the gray windows, she could see the clouds moving wildly across the sky.

And then she thought, *I can't do this anymore.*

She logged out of her computer, left her badge on her desk, and walked out into the sun.

* * * * *

It was one of those days Annapolis gets from time to time when, even though it's located a few hundred miles from the ocean, the air suggests a sea breeze; a hint of salt, possibly spun entirely out of memory, winds in and out of the breezes like a chord in a song. It made her think of Uncle Carl, possibly heading back to the house in Rehoboth at just that moment from Baltimore, ordering a fresh supply of theatrical makeup and getting ready for the season.

As the office building where she'd been working for the last three years of her life shimmered in her rearview mirror, she felt that signs and portents seemed to be all around her. Maybe they always had been. But now she was ready to listen to them.

Molly's husband couldn't understand. To be fair, she couldn't blame him. He yelled a little, and then grew silent. Nothing in his life had prepared him for anything like this. He came from a family of singular ambitions who believed life was like being on a rocket ship. At birth, they would climb in, and then off they would go, incandescent with purpose. Any other course of action baffled him.

Molly felt sorry for him. She didn't mind the yelling. She hoped it made him feel better, but she suspected it didn't. Actually, she realized that she didn't know anything about him, really, and she didn't care all that much that she didn't.

The next morning, she packed up a suitcase and left him a note. *Everything is yours*, it said.

* * * * *

A storm was coming.

Molly looked for flashlight batteries but didn't have any luck. In the kitchen drawers where Carl used to keep them, Molly found only takeout menus and birthday candles, as well as a few sticks of white greasepaint.

Outside the workshop door she paused, the key in her hand. The wind off the water was already fierce. She thought of it as Joe's workshop, even though technically that was not the case. It was now hers, as was the house and everything in it.

She had every right to go inside to look for batteries, she told herself.

As she opened the door, a monster loomed, its head and teeth terrible in the dying light. Lighting made its edges glow, and Molly nearly screamed. Then she calmed down. Remembered where the switch was for the overhead bulb.

She was so amazed at what she saw that she almost forgot to look for the batteries. She'd seen Joe's work before, of course. She and Carl used to go to his shows, help him set up. But it had been a while. Even though he hadn't been staying there long, it looked like he'd started on a number of new projects, or had been modifying old ones. A seven-foot-tall creature with gears for eyes stretched out skinny metal arms. A smaller, feral-looking thing with copper ears gazed back at her, its bicycle-chain tail held at alert.

They were made out of metal, but they looked scared. And haunted. Like they were missing something. Like they were looking for something they had lost.

Molly reached out and touched the cold ribs of an alien skeleton. It was a mystery how anyone could create anything with such feeling infused into it. And an even greater mystery that it was Joe, with whom she struggled to hold a conversation about anything. How was it possible that she could barely communicate with in-person Joe, yet feel these soaring waves of emotion pouring off things he created out of discarded hubcaps and aluminum cans?

Uncle Carl, of course, was a different story. She could talk to him about anything. And he'd been a bridge between her and Joe, although she could sense that Joe wasn't happy after she moved in. She was the wayward niece who had dropped out of her normal life and landed in the midst of their love affair with no visible talents. The only one of the three of them who was not an artist. Although, Molly wondered: If she wasn't an artist, how was it that she could understand what Joe's creatures were communicating, or what Carl was conveying with his eyes and hands when he performed on the boardwalk?

How was it that she could *feel* what they were trying to say, as if she were an antenna and Joe's sculptures and Carl's performances were radiating signals that she pulled out of the air without any effort at all? Whether she always wanted to detect them or not was entirely beside the point.

There were Carl's videos on YouTube, but of course there were other mimes from around the world. And street performers, with acts Molly had never heard of. Performing on streets in countries like France, Italy, Spain, and Japan.

Entire afternoons slid by as Molly watched one video after another. The ghostly audio made her feel that she was there in the crowd. The sound of wind battering against fabric awnings, distant dogs barking. Faraway traffic on its way to unknowable destinations.

She took notes. Drew diagrams.

One weekend, she borrowed Joe's truck, went to a flea market in Dewey Beach, and bought a giant mirror that she hauled home and put in Carl's room, propping it up against the wall. She went to a fabric store in Lewes. She found exactly what she wanted: something silvery and gray, and a little shiny. Thin enough to flutter gently in an ocean wind.

Finally, one afternoon she finished the diagram of what she needed, including the exact measurements, and brought it to Joe in the workshop. Joe was playing a Miles Davis album, turned up as loud as it would go. When she walked in, he frowned under his safety goggles. But he examined the diagram and agreed it would be easy enough. He probably already had most of what he needed to put it together.

"What's this for, anyway?"

Molly waved a hand loosely in the air, but then it drifted to her side. A silver pig with sorrowful eyes was gazing at her from across the workshop. Something about its expression reminded her a little of her uncle Carl.

We both loved him, was what she almost said.

But what she actually said was, "You'll find out soon enough."

She practiced for weeks in Uncle Carl's bedroom with the door closed. Watched every movement she made in the mirror propped against the wall.

* * * * *

It was mid-August when Molly decided she was ready. That desperate time when summer is still real but everyone can feel its haunted, golden nature sliding out of their grasp.

She took her bag of supplies to the spot where Carl used to perform and began to prepare, fitting together the metal pieces Joe had made for her. Sea grass whispered in the wind behind her as she slipped the costume over her head. While she got ready, a family standing in line for ice cream cones looked at her curiously, but no one else seemed to be paying attention.

It was time to start.

At first, it was a few people watching, then about a dozen, and then easily over fifty, all pointing at the silvery figure who appeared to be floating in the air, holding on to nothing but a thin metal pole, her hand resting casually on the top. The folds of her costume glinted in the dazzling afternoon sun. Even though there was no desk or computer actually there, and all of the figure's movements were so small you almost couldn't see them, it was easy to see that she was staring at an invisible monitor and moving an invisible mouse, checking the screen of an invisible phone over and over again for a message that it was clear from the expression on her face had never arrived.

She stayed there for a long time. The wind blew off the ocean. The light faded from the day.

The next day, she came back, and then the day after that. All that summer, and the summers that followed, she did exactly the same thing every day that the weather was nice. She'd never remembered being particularly attached to any one season before. But now, she loved summers. She could tell that the summer visitors were all searching for something; she could see it in their eyes. She understood how that felt. That longing.

Molly believed that Carl had understood this as well. She was as sure of this as if they'd sat down and talked about it. Even if it wasn't a conversation in the strictest sense of the word. More of an understanding that spanned through time.

It's been years now. But people say she's still there.

EMILY ZASADA'S SHORT STORIES ARE FORTHCOMING OR HAVE APPEARED IN *YOUR IMPOSSIBLE VOICE*, *STRAYLIGHT LITERARY MAGAZINE*, *MENACING HEDGE*, *PENNY AND FLOCK* (FORMERLY *FICTION FIX*). SHE LOVES JAZZ, SEVENTIES MUSIC, AND THE COLOR ORANGE. ORIGINALLY FROM THE BALTIMORE AREA, SHE NOW LIVES IN NORTHERN VIRGINIA WITH HER HUSBAND AND SON. SHE HAS A DEGREE IN ENGLISH FROM TOWSON UNIVERSITY. EMILY HAS NEVER BEEN A MIME, BUT ADMIRES ART IN ALL FORMS. HER THEATRICAL EXPERIENCE IS LIMITED TO WORKING ONE SUMMER AT A CHILDREN'S SCIENCE MUSEUM, PERFORMING IN A PLAY ABOUT SPECIAL EFFECTS USED IN THEATRE, AS WELL AS DEMONSTRATING (NOT ALWAYS SUCCESSFULLY) THE SCIENCE BEHIND PULLING A TABLECLOTH OUT FROM UNDERNEATH MULTIPLE PLACE SETTINGS ON A TABLE.

The Fog

By Linda Chambers

Marianne woke Charlotte up at 7:30. "Come on, honey," she whispered, not wanting to disturb anyone else. "Rise and shine."

Charlotte groaned and squished her face into the pillow.

Marianne made sure her daughter was awake, then she loaded the chairs, beach bags, and a small cooler into the trunk of the car. She turned, a bright smile on her face.

Charlotte slouched out of the cottage. She shivered dramatically, pulled her sleeves down over her hands, and climbed into the car.

The traffic was surprisingly light, and Marianne was able to pull into an empty spot on Lake, practically in front of Starbucks. "Wow, that's luck!" she said, opening her door. "What do you want? Coffee? Cold, hot? A pastry?"

Charlotte shrugged. Her phone was already out, her eyes glued to the screen.

Coffee balanced in one hand, Marianne continued into town, where she found a great parking space right on Rehoboth Avenue. "Unbelievable!" she said, counting out quarters. "I wonder where everyone is. . . ."

Charlotte glanced out the window at the overcast sky. No mistaking the sarcastic *"seriously?"* in the arched eyebrow.

Marianne handed Charlotte her bag and towel. "See," she said, "when we're ready for lunch, we can leave our stuff on the beach and walk right up to Grotto's."

Charlotte rolled her eyes and muttered, "Are we going to be staying *that* long?"

That did it. Marianne gathered her own things, slammed the trunk shut, and marched toward the boardwalk, fuming. *Charlotte.* Fifteen years old and insufferable. Bored with the activity, impatient with her mother—that tone, attitude, and expression—put it all together and BOOM! There she was. Yes, it was chilly. Yes, there were some clouds. Yes (she searched her brain for something else to add to the litany but couldn't find it). *Fine.* She'd just go with that.

They crossed the boardwalk and stopped dead at the ramp to the beach.

"Bit foggy out today," Marianne said, after a few beats.

"Understatement," replied Charlotte.

Marianne desperately wanted to snap, "Does *nothing* please you?" Except . . . well, Charlotte was right. It *was* an understatement.

The fog was rolling in off the water—an enormous cloud of it. Dense fog. John Carpenter-film fog. At any moment, a skeletal band of ghostly sailors might emerge from it, swords raised to exact retribution for the terrible crimes committed against them.

"Hey, what does this remind you of?" Marianne asked, and put on her breathiest Adrienne Barbeau voice: "The fog is moving inland, away from the beach, towards Antonio Bay . . . there's something in the fog. . . ."

Charlotte sighed again, adding a shrug to the picture. "Are we doing this?"

Fine, Marianne thought. "Yes," she snapped.

She trudged ahead without consulting her daughter on where to stake their claim. It didn't matter—all the spots were good. Except for the fog.

Marianne barely had time to open her beach chair before Charlotte was prone on her towel, buds in her ears, scrolling through her phone.

The new norm.

Fine, Marianne thought again. Out of the corner of her eye, she saw Charlotte glance at her. Marianne wondered if she had actually said that last "fine" out loud.

Once seated, Marianne looked around.

The fog now shuttered them on all sides. To the left were a few scattered towels and beach chairs. A middle-aged woman in shorts and a turquoise top was bent over a large hamper, sorting through its contents. A young woman in a green paisley bikini was stretched out on her towel, propped up on her elbows, reading a book. Several figures in T-shirts and shorts moved back and forth, disappearing and reappearing in the curtain of gray. She could just make out the lifeguard post and the yellow flag on the pole beside it that indicated dangerous surf. Straight ahead, the ocean rolled up to the shore, white crests and silver sparkles visible only a few yards out. She could see some people splashing close to shore.

Things were a bit more interesting to the right. A large, netted pushcart, stuffed with bags and a cooler, sat in the middle of a circle of chairs of various sizes. Three umbrellas surrounded them, one blue and the other two rainbow-striped. Several towels were spread beneath them. Three buckets—blue, yellow, and red—lay on their sides in the sand. It was haphazard, yes, but there was a definite sense of arrangement. In the distance, she could see faint outlines of people shifting in and out of visibility, but none who seemed actively involved with the beach scene. It had the look of a home hastily abandoned.

She turned to comment on this to Charlotte, but Charlotte was busy texting. Marianne pulled out her paperback, a battered copy of Peter Straub's *Shadowland*. No more attempts to bridge the communication gap, she swore. If Charlotte wanted to sit in silence, if she'd rather text her friends than talk to her mother, well, fine. And again, *fine.*

Charlotte wasn't being punished. She hadn't been dragged to the beach against her will. No one had forced her to cancel plans with her friends. She had, in fact, agreed the night before to accompany

Marianne. She hadn't been jumping up and down with excitement, but then, she never did. Not anymore.

Marianne thought, *I don't care if we get swallowed up in this mess, we'll stay till lunch. That'll show her.*

The fog remained.

Twenty minutes into rereading a page for the third time, a bright splash of color zoomed past her, accompanied by a high-pitched giggle of delight.

"Wait for me!" It was a beach command that all mothers instantly recognized. Instinct had Marianne halfway out of her chair before she focused on the situation.

That bright splash was a tiny girl in a pink tutu, long, brown hair flowing down her back. She skidded to a halt just shy of the water, her arms flung wide, palms up, fingers spread, as though she were getting ready to hug the ocean. It was a gesture of such joy, such *fearlessness,* that Marianne gasped. She couldn't help herself. *Charlotte,* she thought. Charlotte long ago! How many times had Charlotte raced down the beach, hurtling headlong into the waves? Oh, joyful, fearless Charlotte!

"Wait for me!" The voice was firm, but not panicked. Marianne glanced to her right and realized the abandoned household—the Roanoke of the beach—was now filled with activity. A woman was on her feet, ambling toward the water. She was probably thirty, slightly overweight, wearing a stylish suit with a concealing skirt; her hair was caught up in a clasp. Her toes were painted the same bright pink as her daughter's suit.

A wave swirled round the little girl's ankles, and she laughed and twirled and clapped. The tiny ballerina cried impatiently, "Come on, Mom!" and held out a hand. Mom laughed, too, suddenly breaking into a run the last few feet. She grabbed the little girl, now squealing with joy, swept her up in her arms, and ran into the ocean with her.

On a brighter day, Marianne might not have noticed it. That bright splash of pink tulle might have been lost in myriad other colors—bathing suits and towels and buckets and shovels in the sand, water wings and boogie boards in the water, and kites soaring above. The sounds of laughter and splashing and shouting and seagulls would have drowned out a little girl's peal of delight.

Marianne realized Charlotte was sitting up and staring in the same direction. She was grinning.

"Mom, that's *you!*" she said.

Charlotte rose to her feet in one swift movement, yanked the buds from her ears, and dropped them and her phone into her bag. She took off running towards the water, whirling around. "Come on!" she shouted.

Marianne got up with more energy than she expected and raced after her daughter.

Charlotte's arms were raised in triumph. She spun around, her arms wide, palms up, fingers spread.

Marianne and Charlotte joined hands at the water's edge and plunged into the waves together. They laughed with abandon as waves rolled over them.

Neither had noticed that the fog was gone.

LINDA CHAMBERS TEACHES PLAYWRITING AND SCREENWRITING IN THE LITERARY MAGNET PROGRAM AT GEORGE WASHINGTON CARVER CENTER FOR ARTS & TECHNOLOGY IN TOWSON, MD, AND IS AN ADJUNCT FACULTY MEMBER IN STEVENSON UNIVERSITY'S THEATRE & MEDIA PERFORMANCE DEPARTMENT. HER PLAYS HAVE BEEN PRODUCED IN NEW YORK, LOS ANGELES, AND BALTIMORE. SHE IS ALSO A THEATRICAL DIRECTOR AND WORKS FREQUENTLY IN THE BALTIMORE AREA. SHE LOOKS FORWARD TO SPENDING TIME EACH SUMMER ON THE DELAWARE BEACHES.

Too Many Hemingways

By Joseph L. Crossen

I never should have bought that Hemingway.

I couldn't afford it—that was for sure. And it had no place, really, in my business. I'm a bookseller, a vanishing breed. I have a small bookstore in what is a great location in the summer and, lately, not bad in the fall and winter. I'm just a block off the beach on Rehoboth Avenue. I'm hardly getting rich, but there are still folks who haven't fallen for electronic books, who still like, as I do, the heft and smell and feel of a good, old-fashioned book. My little store is comfortable. The Wi-Fi is free, and I brew the coffee fresh. I'm a hardcore coffee addict, so you know it's good. You can have coffee and soda bread or a scone—both homemade—and relax at a small table or in an easy chair. My goal was to own a bookstore that smelled like books and fresh, strong coffee when customers entered. I succeeded.

But I overdid it with the Hemingway. My business is books for folks to read at the beach. I don't have rare editions or collectibles. I am not a collector. Yet, if you asked one of those silly "What book would you take to the moon with you?" kinds of questions, I would quickly say, *The Old Man and the Sea* by Ernest Hemingway. Papa.

The first time I read the book, I was in junior high, and I was sure I'd hate it. In seventh grade, I pretty much hated everything, saving my deepest hatred for anything from an adult, particularly an adult who was a teacher. I never let Miss Packer, my English teacher, know how much I loved that book.

Over the years, if there was nothing good to read, there was always my tattered paperback of *The Old Man and the Sea.* As I grew, the book grew. It meant more to me as time went on, like a favorite old song. Songs we love tend to stick in the time and place we first heard them. Books, though, grow and develop as we do. As we mature, the words on the page remain static. It's our understanding of what lies beneath them that changes.

Now in my forties, my love affair with books has gone on for decades. I was blinded by that love when I saw a first edition, signed copy of *The Old Man and the Sea* in a small, musty bookstore on Newbury Street, while on vacation in Boston. It was a hardbound copy, of course, with a wonderfully simple illustration on the paper dust jacket that depicted a sand-colored fishing village on a hill. Behind it, only the blue sea and sky. Across the top, simply "HEMINGWAY," in all caps, and in all caps across the bottom, "THE OLD MAN AND THE SEA." A man of such simple, crisp writing must have approved of that plain, clean cover art.

Like a kid, I pressed my forehead against the store window. A small card under the book read "Signed First Edition." My heart rate increased. I could feel it climb. I calmed myself with deep breaths. Had someone else seen it and maybe beat me to it? No, I was the only person transfixed by the little novel, and I had to have it.

A quaint tinkling bell rang when I opened the door and entered. I turned to the right to look into the display window from the inside. The book was locked behind the glass. I turned back to the store and saw tables stacked with books and several rows of dark, wooden bookshelves along the rear wall. A few feet to my right, a man in his fifties, sleeves of his flannel shirt rolled at the wrists, sat reading. He glanced up and smiled at me, then returned to his book. I tried to be nonchalant, not give away my excitement, so I strolled slowly among the tables, looking at mysteries and thrillers—my favorites—before moving on to history and bestsellers. Then I drifted toward the man at the counter. "May I see the Hemingway you have on display in your front window, please?" I asked.

I noticed he had a name tag that read "Carl Walton." Mr. Walton closed his book, smiled, and said that I should go to the restroom, wash and thoroughly dry my hands, and then he'd let me handle the book. When I came back, he didn't press me or ask if I was interested in buying the book. He simply reached into the display and handed it to me.

Hemingway had held this book, at least for the time it took to sign it. I opened it gently, and there was his signature. "Ernest Hemingway," signed as straight and as straightforward as the man's prose.

"Mister Walton—"

"Call me Carl, please," he said.

"Carl, is this book for sale?"

"It is, and it has excellent provenance." He handed me a notarized letter detailing the book's ownership history. We talked about the price with minimal negotiation, and I wrote him a check for $7000.

Back in Rehoboth, I debated what to do. Should I lock it in the safe? Put it in a temperature-controlled environment? Display it?

I decided to schedule a celebration to unveil my signed first edition of *The Old Man and the Sea*. A novel that meant so much to me must have meant much to others.

I set to planning, scheduling the event for a day in October. I love our tourists, but tourists bring children, and children are not good for valuable first edition books. I would set the air conditioner at sixty-five degrees. It would be chilly, but the book would be safe from humidity. I arranged for two security guards and planned an area in the middle of the store where I could display the book. I could place a three-foot-high picket fence I used for children's book displays around it. Once I had the details clear in my head, I put out the word to the local book clubs, libraries, and literati.

When that Saturday in October came, I saw I had neglected to consider two things. First, there was the impact of social media. I don't use it, but others do, and word of the showing spread on Facebook and Twitter and God knows what other demon-spawn social media is out there. The good news is that there was a thick line of people waiting for me to open the doors. This brings me to the second thing I failed to consider. I was aware of the existence of Elvis impersonators. I did not know there were such things as Ernest Hemingway impersonators, but apparently there are, and they use social media. They flocked to my store.

As the poem goes, *what to my wondering eyes should appear* but dozens of Ernest Hemingways. I opened the door to a herd of Hemingways, dozens of burly, bearded men, some wearing long-billed fishing caps, all dressed for safari. The Hemingways bumped and shoved by my regular customers. "Daughter," several said. "Where did you put my book, Daughter?" said one. They filled my small store. Hemingways all around.

I've said my store is a small one. With all the Hemingways, there was precious little room for other customers, but the customers seemed to be enjoying the presence of the Hemingways. Imagine being tapped on the shoulder and turning to hear, "Happiness in intelligent people is the rarest thing I know." I heard one tell an elderly gentleman, "The world is a fine place and worth fighting for." Spotting a reporter who was making notes, one of them sidled up to him and said in a tone of advice, "There is nothing to writing. All you do is sit down at a typewriter and bleed." This to a kid who may never have seen a typewriter. "All things truly wicked start from innocence," a leering, Groucho-imitating Hemingway said to an attractive young woman.

I made my way through the crowd welcoming people, Hemingways included. The Hemingways seemed very happy to be there. I made sure the security guards at the entrance and back exit were in position. Then I headed for the center of the store where *The Old Man and the Sea* was on display. People were thick around the book. Hemingways were jostling others to get a look at "their" book. I could feel an electric urge among the onlookers to stretch over the fencing and take hold of the book, touch it, feel something Ernest Hemingway had once held and signed. The way I had it showcased was with the cover removed and spread open, the book open to the frontispiece where the great writer had signed it.

I spent a few minutes answering questions about the book: Where did I find it? Where did my love for Hemingway come from? Do I plan to sell it and, if so, for how much? Afterwards, I told the group it would be nice if they would move on and let others get close to the book. "There are several Hemingway titles you might be interested in over there," I said, pointing to the "American Authors" section.

One gentleman, one of the Hemingways, was slow to leave. I touched his sleeve and suggested he come back to the display once everyone had cleared away. To have to usher a Hemingway through my store, while surrounded by other Hemingways, was a surreal experience I never expected.

I had planned on being open from one to three. Sales of Hemingways and other books were going very nicely. "What a lovely autumn afternoon at the beach," a woman was saying to me, when someone shouted, "It's gone! The book is gone!" I made my way to the display. Sure enough, my prized book was gone. Missing. Stolen.

I shouted, "Everyone, stay where you are. Security, no one is to leave. Clerk, call the police."

"Let's all be calm," I told the group. "If you have the book, please just give it to me now, no questions asked, and everything will be fine. I won't file charges." My heart was beating faster than when I first saw the book. All that money spent just to have the book stolen the first time it was shown in public.

"Please, everyone. Where is the book?" I looked around. I tried to make eye contact with each person, Hemingways as well as regular customers. "Please give me the book."

Nothing. I scanned the crowd again. People looked concerned. They looked confused. Some looked frustrated that they were being retained.

I glanced at one of the Hemingways and stopped. Something about him reminded me of someone else. *Of course.* In college, I had a part-time job with a cleaning service. Most of it was boring (offices) or gross (doctors' offices), but one was interesting—a local television station. I remembered the station manager. His name was Ralph-something, and he worked like a slave at being a calm, smiling, everything's-under-control boss. He worked so hard at maintaining an aura of calm, I felt he would burst. But when someone disagreed with him or an area wasn't cleaned to his liking, he was still calm, smiling, and everything's under control, with one—no, two—exceptions: his ears. Smiling, calm, and controlled all over except for the tips of his ears, which burned a cherry red. I remembered thinking, "How I'd like to play poker with you. Your ears would signal every hand, good or bad."

There was that tell, again, but this time, the bright-red ears belonged to a Hemingway with a long-billed fishing cap atop them. He looked down when I made eye contact. Even with the crowd, I got to him faster than he could get away from me if he had tried.

A nervous smile, then, "And what can I do for you, Daughter?" This was a nice touch because it was the honorific "Papa" Hemingway used for women of whom he was fond, such as Ingrid Bergman. The other Hemingways were focused on this exchange.

"Don't give me that 'daughter' crap," I said. "I'm not Ingrid Bergman, and you're certainly not Ernest Hemingway. Where is my book? Is it on you, somewhere?"

His eyes shifted very slightly to the right, toward the "Half Off" bin of slightly damaged books, and he said, "My book, Daughter, not yours. My book."

"It's not your book. It's mine, and you are trying to steal it. You took it, didn't you? Stole it from the display, right?" I was angry now. Who did he think he was, trying this on me, stealing the book I loved and had paid so much for? I took him by the sleeve and pulled him toward the sale bin. "Did you hide it in here?" I said this while pointing at the sale bin.

"It's my book," he said, again. "I wrote it."

By now, one of the security guys had made his way to us. "Hang on to him, and don't let him go while I look for the book," I told the guard. Then I started down through the bin, pushing books to the sides while I looked for my book. It wasn't there. He'd fooled me with that glance toward the bin.

"Do you have it? Where is the book? You're going to sell it, aren't you?"

He looked at me as if I'd said something confusing. "No," he answered. "I took it because you missed the point." He stretched his arms to include everyone. "All of this misses the point. You don't know what's important."

I saw the Rehoboth Police car pull up to the store, and two officers strode through the front door.

"I know what's important. My book and the fact that you stole it. That's important. Where is it?" He looked at me and shook his head sadly, as if I were a slow-witted, disappointing child.

The cops made their way to us through the Hemingways, looking slightly confused. "The taller cop said, "What's the problem here?" Both cops looked around at the crowd.

"This man stole a valuable book."

"No, no. I just want you to see what's important," the guilty Hemingway said. He looked at the two policemen, "That's all." He said this as if stating an obvious, accepted truth.

"What is your name, sir?" the taller cop asked the thief.

"Ernest Hemingway," he said.

This produced grumbling and muttering from the other Hemingways.

"I mean today. Today, I'm Ernest Hemingway."

"Who are you on other days?" the shorter cop asked.

No response.

"Did you take the book?"

"Well, in a way, I suppose."

"Where is the book, sir?"

"I don't want to say. There are more important things here."

They searched him and, not finding the book, said, "You're going to have to come with us, sir. We'll go to the station and figure this out. Do you have your other identification?" And to me, "You can come to the station at your convenience and file charges."

The Hemingway shook his head. The police took him, each by an arm, and led him away toward their car. The crowd parted to let them through. The other Hemingways looked at him with disappointment as he and the cops went through, and a few bearded heads shook. The customers, dressed in beach casual, looked—some of them—pleased to have this story to tell when they got back at their beach houses.

As the cops walked him to the front door, the Hemingway turned his head and shouted over his shoulder, "That book. It's just paper and ink, binding and glue. It's the words, Daughter. It's the ideas, the images." And then he shouted louder, "It's a man overcoming!"

I saw the Hemingway look back one more time as he was guided into the back seat of the cop car.

Exhausted, and out a signed first edition—my first prize in a collection I had hoped to build—I announced we were closing. People drifted out. The security guys checked each person to be sure the book didn't leave the store. When the Hemingways and the customers were gone, I paid the security guards and the clerk.

I proceeded to scour the store for my book. Everyone had been searched, so it couldn't have left the store. Going shelf-by-shelf and book-by-book was tedious, but I was determined to find *The Old Man and the Sea*. While in the "Graphic Novel" section, an idea struck me: If this imposter really knew Hemingway.... I went to "Fiction" and found the section devoted to F. Scott Fitzgerald, a fellow expatriate and drinking pal of Hemingway's in the Paris of the 1920s. There it was, *The Old Man and the Sea*, standing right between *Tender is the Night* and *The Great Gatsby*. My thief had a sense of history and a need to put Hemingway where he belonged.

I put my arms around the book and slumped into a chair in the reading corner. Old man Santiago lost his great fish to sharks in Hemingway's tale. Mine did not get away. I decided there were no charges to file.

JOSEPH L. CROSSEN HAS PUBLISHED SHORT FICTION IN *THE BROADKILL REVIEW*, *THE FOX CHASE REVIEW*, AND *THE CAPE HENLOPEN ANTHOLOGY 2015*, AS WELL AS *THE BEACH HOUSE* AND *THE BOARDWALK*, BOTH COLLECTIONS OF SHORT STORIES BY LOCAL WRITERS. HIS STORY "THE ARTIST'S STAIN" TOOK FIRST PLACE IN THE 2014 REHOBOTH BEACH READS SHORT STORY CONTEST. "TOO MANY HEMINGWAYS" DEVELOPED FROM A COMBINATION OF WANTING TO WRITE ABOUT A BOOKSTORE AT THE BEACH AND WONDERING IF THERE WERE AS MANY GAGGLES OF HEMINGWAY IMPERSONATORS AS THERE ARE OF ELVIS. JOE LIVES IN DOVER, DE.

Not in My World

By Kathleen Martens

Dee swam away from me. I knew I'd never see her again. I treaded water near the boat where my colleagues slipped her from the canvas sling. She arched her sleek, tapered body, dove down, and slapped a goodbye twice with her flukes, washing me in her wake. I could see the pod of dolphins she would join just a few hundred yards offshore. After three years of pure joy, my aching loss began.

This was the way it should be; it was what I'd worked for, wasn't it—to release her into the ocean where she would migrate and live naturally in the wild with her adopted pod? I'd given three years of my life to prepare Dee for hers, determined not to turn her into a pet, dedicated to protecting her from too much human influence, but that didn't stop the gripping in my chest.

I would never know what had happened to her mother, or what tragedy brought her newborn calf into my life that day. But my time with Dee had changed me, made me realize why I'd spent those long years studying, just for a chance to make a difference. It was no longer about books, research, and a graduate degree in marine mammal communication; it was about one tiny orphan dolphin that had stolen my heart.

* * * * *

Exactly three years before that May release day, I'd found the bottlenose calf, gritty yet alive, on the St. Augustine beach, rolling and flapping in the foam with her pulsing little blowhole, no mother in sight. She couldn't have been more than days, maybe hours, old, measuring about four feet, an average-size calf, with a visible vestige of her umbilical cord.

Think, *think*. This isn't a lab pool; this is real, Deb, I'd told myself. "It's all right little one, it's all right."

I had left my phone in my car for my run; was alone on the beach; couldn't call for help. I'd talked to comfort her, then washed the sand from her body and from around her fearful eyes until she was smooth again. That sleek feel of those special cetacean creatures. Realizing she was too heavy to pick up, and not wanting to jeopardize losing her, I'd immediately put one foot on either side of her, bent over, scooted my hands beneath her, and guided her forty-pound body a few feet deeper into the water. Her only chance was for me to walk her two miles along the shore through the calm surf to the rehabilitation center. I'd learned about the challenges of rehabilitating and releasing captive dolphins; still, I couldn't have known what was ahead—for me, for the calf.

Walking her out a bit deeper, I'd stroked her glossy, rubberlike hide, put my face near the water, and created my signature whistle—a call she would associate with me and eventually try to imitate, a call I hoped would comfort her, an essential vocalization we would use to communicate while I rehabilitated her before reintroducing her into the wild again off the Florida coast.

Click click whistle whistle click ah-ah-ah-ah-ah.

I'd made up an inspired, awkward, vocal pattern that would replace her mother's call. So many recorded versions of dolphin-speak from my lab work were fresh in my memory. Petting her and repeating my signature whistle over and over—as her mother would have done—we made progress down the coast. Too young to vocalize, she'd opened and closed her mouth as though telling me about the tragedy that had befallen her.

The sex of the newborn dolphin would be determined at the center, but I somehow knew the calf was female. "I'll call you Dee."

That delightful, perpetual smile on her upturned beak enchanted me. The flattened, lateral crease on her forehead made her look as if she were thinking about her uncertain future. She'd nodded her head in agreement, opened and closed her mouth, at first silently, days later, talking to me, releasing chatters, chirps, and a laugh—I swear. Was this really happening the first week of my internship at the St. Augustine Marine Life Rehabilitation Center?

Floating on my back, I'd kicked with one arm wrapped under her belly, the other stroking her pliable—soon to become firm—dorsal fin as she pushed us along with her flukes. I held her to my chest and, I confess, I fell in love.

* * * * *

When I arrived at the center with Dee, soaking wet in my running shorts and T-shirt, calling and waving for help with one arm around the dolphin calf, my boss, Jim, was amazed. The dozen team members opened the net to the protected, open-water training lagoon and went into overdrive to save the calf, as the adult female dolphins encircled her, vocalizing support.

"She's in good shape. Nice work, Ms. Sheridan."

"Can I work with her, Jim, please?"

"Not our policy with interns, Deborah. You'll be gone in a month, then what?"

I was already so attached, and she was imprinted on me. I couldn't imagine not helping her survive and find her way back to the tides and tastes of the ocean to join a group of her own. It was a marine biologist's dream challenge.

"What if I stayed and worked for free until she's ready?" I'd blurted out the words before I'd considered the consequences—my fiancé

Rob's feelings, the likely crimp in our still unsettled wedding plans, or my new job commitment to MERR, the Marine Education Research and Rehabilitation Institute in Lewes, Delaware. I'd forgotten almost everything, but I'd remembered that in the wild, nearly forty percent of newborn dolphins die. And I couldn't forget the look in those flickering, frightened calf's eyes.

"New calves nurse over a year. Five or six times an hour. You remember that, right?"

My look must have melted Jim's seasoned heart. He was folding. I must have been crazy. I wasn't hearing anything; I was only seeing the calf, thriving in the ocean, leading a natural life. It just felt so right to me. I was in for the long haul.

"We're talking two, maybe three years of 24/7 until release. Sure you've got this?"

"I can be professional. I know cetacean cow habits, calves, too. I can do this." Honestly, the realities didn't really register at the time, just my instincts.

"OK, but no falling in love with the calf. Could break your heart, you know."

Too late, I should have said. I knew he was right. I had already learned firsthand what we'd learned in school—it was human instinct to romanticize a relationship with a dolphin, especially a little calf with a permanent smiling face. I would ensure Dee remained a wild dolphin with her natural instincts intact.

I wore a waterproof, continuous-loop recording device to broadcast my constant signature whistle, mimicking the repetition a dolphin mother would use to bond with her calf. After five days, Dee had imitated my call, pushing the sounds from her complex nasal passages through her blowhole; after one month, she'd created a unique acoustic signal all her own. Dee's imitation of my call was missing a whistle, a click, and an ah-ah. I smiled. So much to understand about the soundings, or was it the language, of those bottlenose beauties.

If she'd had any chance of being released into her natural world, I would need to avoid reinforcing behaviors that were entertaining to humans or any behaviors unnatural to her. Behaviors she learned from me that weren't true to dolphins would only have to be extinguished later. It was a disciplined, fine line to ride. Stay close, observe, nurture, yet stay detached, blend in.

I stayed with Dee all day, through that night, and the next. I camped out at the center on a cot while the veterinarians checked her and taught me how to feed her. When I offered her the bottle, her tongue curled around a rubber nipple designed to replicate her mother's teat. Little finger-like projections on her tongue locked in like a zipper to keep the milk shake-thick nutrition from spilling into the water. I fed her underwater, just as she would have suckled from her mother, short bursts, as dolphin calves do. Only five-second stints of voracious nursing and we were off parallel swimming, her body tucked in close to mine. Then ten minutes later, she'd be back nursing again. It made me happy to see her begin to swim and toss seaweed with the other young dolphins.

I couldn't wait to go home to our apartment on the seventh day, just to tell my fiancé Rob in person about this miracle in my life. Dee was feeding a little less frequently then; I had a colleague fill in, but I couldn't leave her for long. Rob had just returned from a week away on business. He'd seemed less than excited on our phone calls, listening politely. I knew once I explained, he'd be amazed.

He wasn't.

"I know it's a sacrifice for us, but the time will fly." Rob wasn't buying it. "We have our whole lives . . . and you're always on the road anyway."

"Two to three *years?* You'd jeopardize everything for . . . a damn fish?"

"Dolphins are mammals. Dee's not a damn fish, she . . ."

"*Dee?* What about *me?* Our wedding, your job. Have you lost your mind?"

"Rob, I thought you understood my work, I thought you would . . ."

"You thought I would what? No, Deb, you *didn't* think."

The sound of the door slamming after two weeks of unending arguments stunned me. The morning of our breakup, I was shaking, questioning what I had done. But *a damn fish*—those words made me realize that Rob understood nothing about me at all. Three years together, hearing me talk about my work, my passion, and he knew nothing. Why I'd thrown everything up in the air sky-high like confetti for a *damn fish,* I didn't know. But I was learning things about myself—what *I* needed.

The day Rob left me, Dee bumped up against my side all day long. Was she sensing my pain? Jim must have, too. He went to bat for me, made a call to MERR. They'd have a job for me when I was free. I moved my things into a small apartment near the center, and set up my cot in a screened tent by the water's edge. Now I could focus on Dee's rehabilitation.

At first, when I swam, Dee folded in body-to-body beside me and drafted in my slipstream, a behavior essential for a calf to keep up with the pod. Barely eighteen inches longer than her, and sixty pounds heavier, I wasn't much help. I laughed. My human speed was slowing Dee down. Even as a baby, her burst speed was five miles per hour; later, she'd accelerate to ten or twenty. *I* ended up drafting on *her*. As she grew more powerful, she swam with a mature female dolphin who had lost her calf. But Dee always circled back to me. How could I stay detached?

I never felt lonely after Rob left. I had so many like-minded colleagues for company, and I was focused on coaching Dee to hunt fish, navigate, and communicate—skills she would need to survive in the wild. I hid behind a blind so she wouldn't associate me, *the feeder,* with the fish. Starting with dead fish, I fed her underwater through a submerged plastic tube. She ate voraciously. Then I served a combination of dead fish and live. One day, I released a live, shimmering fish from behind the blind. Dee dove, lunged, and caught it. Victory.

I found ways to use Dee's sonar capability to teach her echolocation—bouncing sounds off objects to identify distance and size—a skill she could use to avoid the deadly propellers of boats and to socialize with other dolphins. I followed all the protocols; she learned fast.

At the center, we were philosophically aligned, similarly dedicated marine biologists. We weren't trainers. Dee was never a toy, never on display to visitors—no hoops, no entertainment, no tossing dead fish in the air. There were only dolphins—and humans who tried to be part of the dolphins' natural scene. To be intimate, yet detached, to avoid applying your human instincts became a Zen-like challenge for me.

* * * * *

"Great work, Deb." Jim stood by the edge of the lagoon.

"Three years. Unreal, right?" Dee popped up next to me. "I figure another year or two and . . ." I could see his face said otherwise.

"It's time, Deb."

"But I still haven't . . ."

"I'll arrange the release boat." He turned to leave. "It's to your credit, you know. Record time."

Dee slipped in front of me and turned over, floating, showing off ribs with a healthy layer of blubber. My throat closed. I ran my hand over her silky belly and looked up at Jim. He understood. Dee flipped over, nudged me, and gave that open-mouthed smile.

It killed me. "Yeah, I know."

* * * * *

As Dee's glistening body disappeared into the horizon with her new group the following week, a mere shadow against the kaleidoscopic early evening sky—the kind of sky that looks like a child's painting, broad brush strokes of rainbow colors—I felt a deep satisfaction and a deep loss. Dragging my feet through the sand, I went home to pack for my job in Lewes, Delaware. My colleagues had painlessly freeze-marked the letter "D" on Dee's dorsal fin. They would track her whereabouts and keep me advised.

No surprise at the depth of my connection with that little creature. I'd worked hard not to jeopardize Dee's release; I felt good about that, and sad for my departure from Florida.

*****

I rented a weathered cedar cottage, silver gray like Dee's gleaming back, in Rehoboth Beach, just a short ride from my job rescuing turtles and injured waterfowl at MERR. Running the mile-long boardwalk daily after work, I always searched the horizon for dolphins. It was common to see them swimming and emerging amid the swells offshore in the late afternoons. After two years, no matter how hard or far I ran, whether my feet pounded the boardwalk or wet sand, I couldn't outrun the loss. An unexpected pressure pushed against my eyes now and then when I scanned the water's surface.

Then I received a call while I was running one morning. Dee had been spotted just south of Ocean City, Maryland, down the coast from Rehoboth. Hugging myself, I could see her wide-open smile in my mind. Those early years with Dee all rushed back. I paced the beach.

On a blazing, sunny, late afternoon two days later, I saw a pod of dolphins unusually close to shore. They were feeding in the cool water on a bait ball—a school of frenzied fish—the dolphins bobbing, circling, and bursting through the surface, excited by their find. I ran with shivers through the cool June waves and began to swim with the tide. I was a skilled swimmer; I could reach them and get back to shore easily. Checking every few strokes, I could see they were still in sight. As I neared them, an unseen current pulled me toward the pod. I was so close, and my instinct took hold at the sight of them. I called out over the water, bubbles tickling my face as I made my signature whistle, *click click whistle whistle click ah-ah-ah-ah-ah,* hoping it would cause some curiosity and draw a few nearer to me.

Then it took hold—the rip current I had ignored. I swam parallel to the shoreline toward the dolphins to release myself, but the tide pulled me farther out to sea. I was tiring. I knew what to do. I gulped a breath, let go, and let it take me. On my back, eyes to the sky, I prayed I would have the strength to swim to shore once outside the rip current.

I dove down to check the movement of the water below, and an undercurrent took me fast, tumbled me. I released my breath in spurts of bubbles that rose toward the glittering surface above. The constriction in my chest became unbearable, tighter, threatening an explosive discharge of what little oxygen I had left. I was in trouble. It wasn't the first time I'd lost all judgment when it came to those beautiful creatures.

A powerful thrust. A rogue wave? My head hit a solid object and things went murky. I was disoriented. What could possibly have. . . . My hands grasped the edge of something unstable—rocking. A wave dunked me under again and I rose up, gasping to fill my lungs with a swallow of briny air. Then I was eye level with a pair of large feet attached to tanned, muscled legs, connected to a tall, fit body with strong arms, who fought to balance his paddleboard. I looked up at his shocked face; I tried to stop my gasping, couldn't speak.

"Hey, you OK?"

Chest still heaving, I sputtered, "I'm . . . fine."

"*That* was amazing." His square jaw hung open, a swath of dark, wet hair draped across his face. He struggled to level out his board.

"What, me trying to outswim a rip current?" I choked out a laugh.

"Damn, I've never seen anything like it. I'm here, day after day, trying to get close to them like that." He reached out his hand, helped me slide up onto the center of the board, and sat facing me, crossed-legged. "Hi. I'm Brian."

Before I could introduce myself, he bolted upright. "He's *back!* Behind you, quick, look."

By the time I looked behind me, there wasn't anything to see, but I felt a slithering under the board and it lifted, like a swell was passing beneath us. Then I heard it, *Click whistle click ah-ah-ah.* The sound shot down my spine, electrified me, and Dee lunged up over the board, wanting to be part of the fun. She circled around us and came to my side, nudging my hand. I burst into tears and laughter at the same time. She opened and closed her beak, rapid fire, and gossiped in squeals and whistles through her blowhole, as though telling me everything that had happened since we'd parted.

"Is this for real?" My new paddleboarding friend leaned over. "This is my dream, seriously." Brian ran his hand down Dee's uplifted beak. "Hi, Buddy." Then he looked at me. "What are you, a dolphin whisperer? I'm blown away. Who *are* you?"

I laughed and hugged Dee's head. "Me? Deb; she's named Dee, a female dolphin I worked with in Florida."

"Florida? Hi, Dee. You're too pretty to be called 'Buddy,' right?" Brian stroked Dee's head again. "You've come a long way." He smiled at me. "Feel this; she's so smooth."

I laughed. "Yes, I know." I looked into Dee's eyes—so many memories, so much emotion. I wanted to be selfish, cherish a few more moments, but I was filled with my original determined dream: I wanted her to be what she was, a dolphin, in her own world, accepted and thriving in the wild. Had my spontaneous signature whistle ruined my years of hard work?

Nearby, I could see Dee's group dispersing, moving one by one, two by two, toward the south, leaving the stirring waters as the bait ball was depleted. She backed away, clicking and whistling, half her body suspended above the water. Then Dee submerged, rose up, turned, and dove again. The last thing I saw was the tracking mark, the letter "D," as she made her second plunge and disappeared. The last thing I heard was her clicking, whistling signature call that had captivated me years before. I tightened my jaw, stopped my instinct—not daring to repeat my own patterned whistle. I couldn't risk her returning to my call, couldn't jeopardize the delicate transition she'd made to bond with her adopted family.

Brian and I both stared in silence, breathing in the balmy salt air, watching the flashes of the slick backs of the dolphins in Dee's pod as they stitched their way down the coast against the vibrant late sky. With water lapping at the sides of the paddleboard, our bodies rocking left and right with the rolling waves, we searched for Dee. We didn't speak until the houses blocked the sinking sun behind us, the shafts of late daylight disappeared, and night had nearly drawn a shade down across the navy-blue chop.

Brian shifted to his knees, lifted his paddle, then stopped in midair, staring out toward the horizon. "Is there anything more beautiful?"

"Not in my world."

"Mine either."

And I knew he understood.

KATHLEEN L. MARTENS IS AN ACTIVE MEMBER OF THE REHOBOTH BEACH WRITERS' GUILD. HER FIRST BOOK, A MEMOIR, *REALLY ENOUGH, A TRUE STORY OF TYRANNY, COURAGE AND COMEDY*, WAS WRITTEN WITH MARGARET ZHAO, A SURVIVOR OF THE CULTURAL REVOLUTION UNDER CHAIRMAN MAO. SHE OWES MUCH OF HER RECENT PUBLISHING SUCCESS TO THE CAT AND MOUSE PRESS REHOBOTH BEACH READS SHORT STORY CONTESTS: "MOLTING" WON A JUDGE'S AWARD FOR *BEACH DAYS*, 2015, AND "FLIGHT OF THE SONGBIRD" WAS FIRST-PLACE WINNER IN *BEACH NIGHTS*, 2017.

She went on to win first place in the Delaware Press Association Communications Contest for best single short story statewide, and second place nationally for a single short story from the National Federation of Press Women. Her short story, "The Beautiful Present: The Gift of Living in the Moment," was published in the May 2017 issue of *Delaware Beach Life*. Most recently, Martens was engaged as the literary arts curator and editor for *The Divine Feminine: An Anthology of Seaside Scribes*, and two new short stories were included in the anthology, *Rehoboth Reimagined*, published by Delaware's Rehoboth Beach Writers' Guild in June 2017.

Judges' Comments

This is one of those rare short stories that taught me something even as it kept me entertained. Clearly, the author knows something about dolphin biology, and, more important, knows how to weave that knowledge into a storyline without losing the narrative thread. The author immerses the reader into a unique world in which nature and humans come together in an unforgettable way, as well as being able to deliver the subtleties of love and heartbreak succinctly and without cliché.

The Bomber Jacket

By Jackson Coppley

Brown leather, cracked with age, yet still supple after all these years, first worn by a man of the greatest generation in war, later acquired by a young boy to appease a passing style, and now hanging here in a consignment shop on Second Street in Rehoboth Beach, Delaware. The embroidered patches spoke its heritage: 827th Bomber Squad on the back, the Flying A on one shoulder, and Old Glory on the other. But setting this one jacket apart from any other, a red Maryland Terrapin pin. The ornament took my breath away. That pin, I put on this jacket many years ago. Holding the jacket to my face, I smelled the salt and smoke of that night in Dewey.

He was so young, or so it seems now when everything becomes younger as I get older. Dark-green eyes, black hair, and a swagger that made him seem taller than he was. He wore this bomber jacket over a white tee, more prideful in the latest fad than to stay warm in the cool weather of spring break at the beach. His swagger put me off, but his charm won me over that spring. So cool, so confident, he drew me in.

Walking with him made the delights of the boardwalk more delightful. Dolles popcorn was heaven's manna; a burger from Gus & Gus, fine mignon; the odd flavors of The Ice Cream Store became culinary exploration. His irresistible laugh made me love him. It was deep, exposing no care in the world.

"What do you want to do in life?" I asked.

"Everything," he answered.

I was sure he would. How I remember the unlimited possibilities, the adrenaline rush of what might be possible when the world is still new to you. If only I could recapture that gold nugget possessed by youth.

We sat by a bonfire on Dewey's beach one dark evening as the short break neared its end. In the moonless sky, the stars over the ocean were magic. Despite the warmth of the fire, I shivered. He took off his prized jacket and placed it over my shoulders. I could not have gotten a more personal token from anyone.

We swore we would stay in touch. No texting back in those days. Just a postcard sent and received now and then. Like all spring romances for the young, forever does not live long. He, like me, must have continued with real life. I never knew. I married, raised kids, divorced, lived on my own. From time to time, I would recall that spring break.

What drew me into this shop, I do not know. I never go to consignment shops. Yet here I am, holding this vestige of the past. It was his bomber jacket. There could be no doubt. The night at the bonfire, I put that pin on his jacket. Something from my school to remind him of me. He said he would keep it there always. It appears he did just that.

I must have held the jacket in my hands too long. A sales girl wanted to know if she could help me. I asked her why the jacket was here.

"Estate sale."

It was a simple answer that spoke volumes. Forever does not live long.

Jackson Coppley is the author of the novel *Leaving Lisa* and the collection of short stories *Tales From Our Near Future*. He writes a daily blog on his website, www.JacksonCoppley.com, where the post "Steve Jobs and Me" won second place for personality profile from Delaware Press Association. A graduate from North Carolina State University in physics, Jack's career spanned senior positions in the Bell System and IBM. Now a full-time writer, he focuses primarily on relationships. "The Bomber Jacket" is a natural expression of that genre. Jack and his wife, Ellen, divide their time between homes in Rehoboth Beach, Delaware, and Chevy Chase, Maryland.

Judge's Comment

I liked the brevity of this tale. With a minimum of words, its author created characters I believed in and a tale that pulled me along. Pretty much word-perfect. And a nice, tight ending.

Ralphie to the Rescue

By Carl Schiessl

I stared across Ocean Drive, over the wooden walkway separating two huge beach houses. I could see only blue sky, but I knew the ocean was there, waiting for us to cross. Grandma, Olivia, and I watched cars speed past, most heading toward Cape Henlopen State Park. Cyclists were heading back from the park after a morning ride. Runners were out in both directions.

"Watch out for the joggers," cautioned Grandma, holding Olivia's hand tightly. "They won't stop for anyone. And they can't hear a thing with those headphones on."

I stood silently, waiting for Grandma to decide to cross. It had been several minutes, and we were still standing there. I could've crossed eight times already. I could be on the beach, but I had to wait for them. I tapped my fingers impatiently on my new Quiet Storm skimboard, staring up at Grandma. I said nothing.

It was my first day back at Rehoboth Beach. My mom and Aunt Amanda were running errands and shopping at the Tanger outlets, while Dad was golfing at the Bayside Resort Golf Club down in Fenwick Island.

I looked up into the blazing, metallic-white sky, trying to locate the sun. I squinted and looked downward at the wispy white clouds, some so thin as to be barely detectable. The sky behind the clouds was an intense light blue, growing darker as my eyes moved closer to the horizon.

It was a short walk from my grandparents' house on Bayberry Drive to the North Shores Beach Club. Just a couple blocks. I turned around and looked at the open parking spaces. Grandma could drive, but she always walked. "You gotta keep moving if you want to stay young," she would say to herself.

Olivia pulled Grandma's hand. "I want to go to *beach*, Grammy." Her big green eyes stared up at her grandmother from under her pale-yellow, floppy hat.

"All right," replied Grandma. "I know it's your first day back. It looks pretty clear. Let's make a run for it. Hold my hand, Olivia."

I burst out into the roadway, staying one step ahead, making sure not to get too far in front of them. Grandma held Olivia's right hand, with her favorite beach chair tucked under her left arm and her giant, cloth beach bag over her left shoulder. That bag held an endless supply of towels, hand wipes, sunglasses, fruit, snacks, lotions, books, magazines—whatever one might need at the beach.

We made it across the road, then up the walkway to the top of the dunes. We stopped to take in the scene. Miles of white, sandy beaches in each direction and ocean as far as one could see. People spread out on blankets and under umbrellas of every color.

Looking to my right, I saw a familiar line of royal-blue umbrellas with wooden folding chairs of the same color and fabric, some occupied and others leaning on umbrella poles. White signs with black letters in clear plastic holders were clipped to the bottoms of each umbrella. They blew in circles in the breeze.

"Let's find our 'brella," exclaimed Olivia.

I chuckled to myself as I watched her start to make a beeline for the first umbrella.

"I'm sure we're in our usual spot," said Grandma. We strolled down from the dune to the hard, wet sand by the water's edge. I walked close enough for the cool water to lap at my feet and stared at the waves gently crashing on the shore. When I took a deep breath, the salt air tickled my nose. A cool breeze blew off the ocean. The waves were pretty small—the tide must be out. Not a day to body surf. I looked down at my skimboard. It would be a good day for wave skimming.

We walked away from the shoreline and up the beach to the line of blue umbrellas. The first three were standing in place like soldiers in formation. Olivia was waiting at the third umbrella. Grandma grasped the plastic cover and read the word SARGENT in bold, black letters.

"Our usual spot," said Grandma happily. There were two beach chairs leaning against the pole. "They got it right," she said, as she handed me a chair.

"I'm gonna say hello to the ocean," said Olivia, as she bolted toward the water's edge.

Grandma looked up. "Carson, would you please keep an eye on your sister?" she asked as she opened and set down her favorite beach chair.

"Sure."

"We'll need to get some lotion on you," she said, pulling a large beach blanket from her bag.

"Do you need help spreading the blanket?" I asked.

"No, I'm fine."

I walked slowly toward the water. Olivia jumped around the wavelets, stepping backward when the water level rose and forward when it receded.

"V, pretty cool to be back at Rehoboth," I said.

"I love visiting Grammy and Papa," she exclaimed.

V was my personal nickname for Olivia. No one called her that except me. She didn't respond to anyone else who used it. She was my only sibling. When she was born five years ago, Mom insisted that everyone call her "Olivia." I was ten years old then and thought the name was too long, so I called her V. Olivia loved it.

"Come get some lotion," called Grandma, as she applied SPF 15 to V's olive-colored skin.

It complemented her thick, dark hair and green eyes.

"Here, Carson," she said, handing me a tube of SPF 50. "Don't forget to put lotion on your feet. Nothing's worse than getting burned toes." My skin was more like my mom's. It was so white that I looked like a ghost. I turned my arms upside down, looking at the blue veins radiating just under the skin. My hands and the top of my forearms were well tanned. Short, golden hairs were visible over my brown skin, but the skin on my upper arms and chest was untanned. Papa called it a "baseball tan." That made sense, since the high school baseball season had just ended.

"Come here," ordered Grandma. "Let me do your back." As I stood with my back to her, she slathered my back with lotion. I looked around uncomfortably. It felt strange having my grandmother put lotion on my back, but it was easier than trying to do it myself.

"How was your first year of high school?" she asked.

"Good."

"Your mom said you kept your grades up and had a pretty good baseball season."

"Yes," I said. "It was a good year."

"How about a girlfriend?"

"No," I replied flatly. I was a high school freshman. The lowest form of life. All the cute freshman girls dated upperclassmen. It was hard to get noticed, but now that freshman year was over, maybe things would change.

"You know Papa wishes he could be here," said Grandma.

"I know." He went to the beach at least once per day. He loved the ocean and being at the beach, especially with his grandchildren.

"Your hair is as blond as his was . . . and your mom's."

After they retired, Papa and Grandma opened an ice cream parlor on Rehoboth Avenue near the Purple Parrot Grill. Papa opened and closed the parlor each day, but he sometimes had to work during busy summer days. I hoped to work there someday.

Grandma put down the lotion and removed a paperback book from her bag. I eyed my skimboard. It was time to hit the water. As I grabbed the board, Grandma called out, "Would you mind taking Olivia down to the water while I read?"

I stopped and thought about objecting, but then dropped the skimboard on the sand. V was already on her feet, looking at me with a big smile. Grandma settled into her beach chair, book in hand.

"No problem."

*****

V pulled a yellow, plastic pail and shovel from Grandma's bag. "Let's build a sand castle, Carson," she shouted, as she stumbled over the uneven sand. I slowly trudged to where V was standing.

"How 'bout here?" she asked, pointing to an open spot along the wet sand line.

"You don't want your castle to be flooded," I said, walking back a few yards. "How about here? The castle won't get wet up here."

"OK," she said, hopping to where I was standing. The white frills on her light-green, two-piece bathing suit bounced up and down, in sync with each hop.

I dropped to my knees in the hot sand. "We're gonna need some water, though. You fill the pail, and I'll start building a mountain for the castle."

"All right," I said, watching as she ran down to the water, dropped her pail into the surf, and pulled it out. I grabbed the shovel and started pushing sand into a mound, then jumped in a circular pattern, pushing sand up onto itself, moving one quarter to the left and pushing up again. Sand flew in every direction. I positioned myself so I could keep an eye on V. Then, from directly behind me, I heard girls laughing. I blushed, assuming they were laughing at my antics. I fell to my knees and slowly looked back, hoping they weren't looking at me.

Two girls were sitting on beach blankets. One, a blonde in a royal-blue two-piece, sat with her long legs stretched over her blanket. The other, a petite brunette, wore a soft-pink bikini. She grasped her knees close to her body and rocked slowly back and forth. They were still giggling. Fortunately, they were not looking in my direction. I sighed in relief, resuming my castle-building, though less enthusiastically than before. I glanced occasionally in two directions, first toward V and then toward the girls. The girls passed their phones back and forth, sharing images and laughing loudly. I hoped it wasn't videos of me playing in the sand.

"Where do you want this?" asked V.

I looked away from the girls and back toward V. She was holding a pail of sandy water. "Huh? Oh, just put it down anywhere," I said. "We'll use it to decorate the walls."

"OK."

I looked back at the girls, who were now applying suntan lotion. I stared at the brunette. She already had a terrific tan. Dark-brown hair with a hint of auburn cascaded over her shoulders and touched the back of her arms. Her smile lit up her face. It looked like she had brown eyes, but it was hard to tell from this distance. I bet she was a local. She couldn't have gotten such a great tan over a few days.

"Carson . . . CAR-SON!" shouted V, breaking my trance. "I'm hot. Let's go swimming." She sped toward the water. I jogged after her, grabbing her from behind and carrying her in. We played in the surf, with me acting like a shark, trying to grab her when she got close. I glanced over at the girls. They were on their feet, pointing out to sea.

Dolphins, I concluded. They had to be seeing dolphins. So I carried V out to waist-deep water, where we put our heads under the surface and listened to the dolphins.

"You can really hear them," said V. "What are they saying?"

"They're just playing," I said. "They're enjoying the beach, just like us."

As I carried V out of the water, I noticed four guys on skimboards, catching rides along the shore. They were hooting and hollering, making alternating runs at the perfectly breaking waves. I stood, watching jealously, wishing I could be with them.

"Put me down," shouted V. Seeing we were safely behind the wave skimmers, I gently placed V just beyond the ocean's reach. We made our way back to the sand castle.

"Do you want to keep building?" I asked.

"No, let's go see Grandma." Off she sped toward the blanket. I picked up the pail and two shovels, glancing over at the girls. They were on their feet, each with an arm wrapped around the other. They kicked their legs in unison, first a half kick, then a full kick. They were laughing aloud, counting out "*one-two-three-four, one-two-three four.*" The blonde had trouble keeping time with the brunette, often stumbling or making the wrong kick. The brunette's movements were in time. She never stumbled. It seemed she was teaching the dance to the blonde. As they continued with their beachside can-can, I stood and stared. Then I heard a commotion behind me. The four skimboarders had noticed the girls and were heading their way. The girls stopped dancing and stood before the boys. They were all smiling and laughing, seeming to know one another. Locals, maybe. Probably Cape Henlopen High School students.

When I reached the blanket, V was already lying under the umbrella. I eyed my skimboard. Maybe it was time to hit the surf. Grandma looked up from her book. "Your mom called," she said. "We have to leave the beach shortly."

"Why?" I asked.

"Your mom and Aunt Amanda are bringing Grotto pizza home for dinner," said Grandma, closing her book. "They got tickets to a play."

"A play?" asked V.

"Yes," said Grandma. "We have tickets to the theater. It's Christmas in July!"

"Christmas in July!" exclaimed V. "That sounds like fun."

"Do you remember Ralphie from *A Christmas Story*? You know, the Christmas movie?"

Olivia looked quizzically at Grandma.

"Don't you remember Ralphie and the BB gun?" I asked, "and the bunny pajamas?"

"Ralphie and Christmas at the beach," sang V gleefully. I looked at my skimboard. My heart sank. I turned away and stared out over the water. My eyes wandered to the two girls. The four skimboarders had gone back to the waves. The girls were lying on their backs, sunning themselves. I stared longingly at the brunette, studying her features, wondering what I would say if I ever had the chance to meet her. But there was no way she would ever be interested in a guy like me.

* * * * *

I followed Grandma, Mom, Aunt Amanda, and V into Clear Space Theatre. Rows of seats surrounded the elevated stage on three sides. Aunt Amanda and Mom sat in the second row, with me, V, and Grandma in front. I didn't want to sit in front, but Grandma insisted that we should have the best view.

A Christmas Story. I liked the movie, but Grandma said this was a musical. The only songs I could remember in the movie were when Ralphie and his family sang "Jingle Bells" and "Deck the Halls" with the waiters at the Chinese restaurant. This was a children's musical, with child performers. Theater kids spending their summers doing plays rather than having fun at the beach. This was going to be an evening of pain. After today on the beach, this was a sad start to my vacation.

Ralphie took the stage. The kid playing him really looked like the actor in the movie. He had a large, round head, straight, blond hair, and dark-rimmed glasses. I liked him. Poor, hapless Ralphie. All he wanted for Christmas was a Red Ryder, carbine-action BB gun. And all he got was grief from his parents, his teacher, Miss Shields, and every other adult with whom he came in contact. I understood his frustration.

Ralphie broke into song about the virtues of his BB gun. His family joined the number, and soon a group of dancers took the stage. I watched as they pranced around the stage, belting out the chorus.

There, on stage, among the actors, were the two girls from the beach. They were dressed as shoppers, in long, 1940s-era dresses with white blouses. They were each holding purses, swinging them in harmony with the music. Other characters held top hats, canes, and shopping bags. I stared at the brunette. Her deep tan stood in stark contrast with the Christmas theme, but otherwise, she fully looked the part of a Christmas shopper. Beach beauty by day, Christmas shopper by night.

I stopped following the plot of the play. I'd seen the movie several times. I knew the story. Instead, I watched and waited for the musical numbers, hoping to see the brunette. In one song, Ralphie pretended to be a hero, saving Miss Shields from scoundrels, pirates, and the evil cowboy, Black Bart.

Cowboy Ralphie

The favorite son of Indiana,

With his gun and his bandana

Riding high

The girls came out in full cowgirl regalia, wearing fringed leather skirts and vests, cowboy hats and boots, their hair tied into long ponytails. I stared at the brunette, following her every move. She was a terrific dancer, always in sync with the music, unlike most of the rest of the group. They were clunky and off time; she was lithe and graceful. And she looked even better with her hair tied back. She danced her way over to her partner from the beach. They joined arms and broke into a can-can dance, just like the one they rehearsed on the beach.

Ralphie to the rescue, oh-oh

Ralphie to the rescue, oh-oh

This time, the girls did not stumble. They executed the dance perfectly, alternating short kicks and high kicks. I found myself clapping enthusiastically after the number. My grandma glanced down at me, smiling.

My brunette danced the lead in every number. She appeared throughout the musical as Ralphie's classmate, a neighbor, and several random characters. Between scanning the stage for her, I found myself pulling for Ralphie, savoring his successes and feeling for him as he relived this special Christmas in Broadway-style songs.

As the play wound to a close, the entire cast joined Ralphie onstage to repeat the song *Ralphie to the Rescue*. She was wearing a soft-pink ballerina outfit with tights and slippers, her dark hair pulled back in a tight bun. She looked like a doll. I watched intently as she danced her way through the now-familiar number with her blonde friend, who was also dressed as a ballerina, but in a powder-blue tutu. They locked arms, laughed, and began dancing the can-can.

Half kicks followed by full kicks. They danced across the stage, repeating the kicks as other characters joined the line. Soon she was dancing directly in front of me. I stared at her, hoping she might look at me. She half-kicked, then leapt robustly into a full kick. As she stretched out her leg, her slipper flew off her right foot, high into the air. I watched it soar upward, rotating slowly forward. The slipper rose and spun, as if in slow motion. It crested and then began its descent, still slowly rotating. I might be able to catch it. I jumped from my seat and stretched my arms high into the air. Reaching as far as I could toward the slipper, I felt my hands close around it.

I stared at the slipper in my hands. I couldn't believe it. I slowly looked up at the stage. She was standing before me, her cheeks flushed and her eyes sparkling. She was smiling—smiling at me.

It was going to be a great summer.

CARL SCHIESSL IS A HEALTHCARE ATTORNEY, LECTURER IN LAW, AND AUTHOR WHO LIVES IN CONNECTICUT BUT SPENDS AS MUCH TIME AS HE CAN AT THE DELAWARE SEASHORE WITH FAMILY AND FRIENDS. THIS STORY WAS INSPIRED BY THIRTY YEARS OF SUMMER VISITS TO THE SARGENT HOUSE ON BAYBERRY LANE, REHOBOTH BEACH. THE AUTHOR DEDICATES THIS STORY TO HIS GRANDSON CARSON, WHO WAS HIS INSPIRATION.

JUDGE'S COMMENT

I have thought about this story again and again because the images of this young boy's world are vivid and true. Mood, the conflict of longing versus responsibility, frustration versus sheer joy, are handled with economy, making the point without being overbearing. The dichotomy of that strange interlude between boyhood and manhood is handled with subtlety. Every detail builds to the climax, which flies in the air like that dance slipper—metaphor now for the startlingly happy, memorable moments we've all known. I love the last line! It makes me smile.

The Swimsuit Issue

By Chris Jacobsen

It was 1964 when *Sports Illustrated* came out with its first swimsuit issue. And I was on the front cover.

It was the end of third grade. My teacher assigned a project that involved cutting out magazine pictures portraying our favorite things. I knew right where to find my parents' stash of mags—stockpiled in the small wicker basket next to the green commode. My nail-bitten fingers flipped through the glossy assortment containing *House Beautiful* and *Better Homes and Gardens,* and then, there it was, a *Sports Illustrated* with a most beguiling cover. I did not know what a beautiful girl in a two-piece bathing suit had to do with sports, but suddenly I knew what I wanted to be when I grew up—her!

As I leave Pennsylvania behind and head down Route 1 to Rehoboth Beach, I cannot wait to cross through the door of the vacation home my sister and I share. Being teachers, we have made a point of having one month of sibling-time each summer, now that our parents have passed away. The laid-back atmosphere of this wonderful beach town has been a refuge to which I look forward every day I am not there. Beckoning me are morning jogs on the sand, meandering bike rides on shaded trails, and strolls on the boardwalk. I love the humble entertainment of eating an ice cream cone while sitting on a bench or listening to an evening concert at the gazebo. But the best part of being in this seaside getaway is lying on the beach with the sun warming my back and my stress receding with the tide. Rehoboth has never failed to cloak me in an aura of health and well-being.

It's painful to think this summer will prove to be the exception.

The breeze through the open car window stirs up the contrast between that child-at-play summer and the ongoing struggle of trying to make peace with my current situation.

Jeez, but that *SI* cover was mesmerizing! Here was my ticket to being beautiful and famous. I would change my blah name to hers and be forever known as "Babette." What could be better than living life in a bathing suit? And being at the beach was my most favorite thing in the whole world.

I enlisted Cindy, my younger sister by eleven months, to be the photographer for my "photo shoot." And what other setting could there be than Hawaii? Immediately, my mind's eye conjured up palm trees sprouting on Rehoboth's dunes and fine, black sand that squished between my toes. Using a camera quite similar in concept to the air guitar, Cindy snapped away as I placed a hand just so on a bony hip and squinted my flecked, green eyes in what I hoped was a sultry look. Kneeling on pale, scrawny legs at the water's edge, my kinky, auburn hair morphed into wind-swept blonde tresses. Cute surfer boys gawked as I kicked up spray, the camera catching the moment crisp droplets of saltwater ricocheted off my bronzed skin. Never did a model pucker up with more lavish lips than mine, painted in alluring Chapstick.

"You look fahh-bu-lous, Beth!" Cindy called out over the cries of the seagulls as I changed poses and facial expressions. She easily could have been my twin, as her wiry hair and gangly limbs reflected back to me.

"It's 'Babette,' Cindy. Get it right." I tugged at my wedgie, which made a wet, sucking noise as it released.

"Okaaay, *Babette,*" she responded, while rolling her eyes.

I threw my arms over my head and arched my back. Foam swirled around my ankles; my feet sunk in the sand. Farther down the beach, little kids shrieked as they ran for safety from the rushing rivulets. Maybe later I would sign autographs.

"Click, click," my dutiful sister intoned, as her finger pushed on the invisible button that operated the imaginary camera. No longer clad in my little-girl suit with ruffles and polka dots, I was stunning in Babette's white two-piece (except mine was purple because that was my favorite color). I even scooped up thick, wet sand and poured it down my top so there would be some outward straining of the fabric across my flat chest.

Today, as my sixty-third birthday looms large, my chest is just as flat.

Last year, I had a double mastectomy. I know how fortunate I am that the cancer was caught at an early stage. And there is every reason to anticipate a complete and permanent eradication. My treatment is over, my energy has returned, and my hair has grown back.

But there is more to recovery than just the physical aspects.

Making the left-hand turn onto Route 1A, I fall into the familiarity of this welcoming town. Its streets are my streets, the shops and their keepers are old companions, and just being by the ocean remains a privilege I've never taken for granted.

I turn off the radio so as not to miss the surround sound of this homecoming: bicycle wheels whizzing, flip-flops slapping, pedestrians chattering, and the clink of quarters keeping the meters fat as they stand sentry over cars neatly parked in angled spaces.

Snippets of my summer of '64 and those that followed hover along the edge of my thoughts. I made it a point, at the end of every school year, to locate the *Sports Illustrated* swimsuit issue in my parents' bathroom. And as I pass each cross street along Rehoboth Avenue, I find I am probing my psyche as to how those summers impacted my self-esteem.

Fantasy is a powerful thing.

It was nice to have a younger sister who could be bossed around, but by the second summer of my "photo shoots," Cindy felt that turn around was fair play. We switched roles, back and forth, model and photographer. Cindy chose Outer Mongolia for her shoot. Neither of us knew if there were beaches there; it sounded exotic and so it worked. I clung to "Babette" as my professional name like an actor reprising a role on stage. Cindy wanted "Barbie" because that had been her favorite doll. I thought it was a dumb choice, but I needed her participation so I kept my mouth shut.

Looking back, being a grade ahead in school, I thought that I would always outpace Cindy. I could stay up an hour later, I was allowed to babysit before she could, and I got my driver's license first. By the time we were in high school, though, things began to change. It was easy to tell we were sisters; we were both tall and slender, had developed nice curves, and had unruly hair that we kept in braids going down our backs. But she was more popular. She played sports, had a fun-to-be-with personality, and exuded an openness that was very inviting. She never lacked for dates.

I, on the other hand, was shy, preferring a good book to a sporting event. I carried around a hefty dose of teenage angst. I lacked self-confidence and hid under big T-shirts and baggy sweaters. It was not until the summer before graduation, while walking the beach in a bathing suit, with large sunglasses rendering me incognito, that I noticed heads turning. Not just those of boys my age, but also of men. At first, I was confused, looking around surreptitiously to see who they were eyeing, because it certainly couldn't be me. But it *was* me. Could I actually be worthy of what those looks implied?

Why did this feel so foreign? Did I, during those summers of make-believe, unknowingly condition myself to accept the notion that any prettiness I had was just a fantasy? Had I, when I outgrew the child's play, suppressed all belief that I possessed any physical beauty? Had I turned my body into that of a recluse? I realized I needed to rethink things.

I began to pay more attention to my appearance. I started wearing makeup and more form-fitting clothing. I started showing a little cleavage. My whole demeanor brightened, and I enjoyed knowing I could be attractive to the opposite sex. I embraced my femininity, which made me a more confident young woman.

As a result, I cherished life and realized I could create my future rather than just being a passenger along the way. I made choices that gave shape to the kind of future I wanted: a teaching degree, career, marriage, and babies. Granted, my divorce was unexpected, and it was when my children fledged the nest, but I was in a good spot, financially and emotionally, until the other sandal dropped. I did not foresee cancer.

And now, I feel as hollow as my old bras.

Without Cindy, navigating my health crisis would have been overwhelming. She was my rock as I went through my chemo—my sandbar when I floundered in deep water. She held me as I cried and made me laugh as only she can do. She allowed me my emotional pain while keeping me from getting lost in it. We went for walks. On the beach, she set up the umbrella and got me nestled into a chair, proffering me a staff recommendation from Browseabout Books. A snug blanket of sound washed over me as the waves pounded the shore, gurgles of glee sprang from excited children, and the boardwalk echoed its parade of life. In the midst of uncertain recovery, Rehoboth continued to bathe my fears with hope that all would be well and I would be restored.

Cindy will be arriving this evening, in time for dinner. I had piled groceries into my little Honda before making the drive down here so I wouldn't have to fight the crowded aisles in the local grocery store. I unload the bags, taking out two steaks, which will go on the grill, snap green beans, and salad fixings. There are also ears of corn to be shucked. A ripe watermelon sits on the yellowed countertop, waiting to be sliced. And multiple bottles of wine. I set the table, surrounded with its four chairs, a chic 1960s ensemble of chrome and Formica. One of these days, the furnishings will get a makeover.

And that's how I feel about myself. The figure that I had—the figure that was sturdy, reliable, and a comfortable fit—is now showing major signs of wear and tear.

For me, getting older came with the usual silent creep: a few more pounds, a bit more flab, wrinkles, and sprinkles of varicose veins. I was never one to think about facelifts or tummy tucks. I have worn my age spots with pride as a testament to wisdom gained, but the cancer threw me for a loop, from which I have yet to straighten out.

I enjoyed dressing to show off my figure, especially once I was confident enough to wear skimpy swimsuits on the beach. I felt feminine, confident, and worthy—worthy of allowing myself to be who I was. It felt so freeing to be able to come out from hiding underneath the layers of clothes, to shout *this is my body;* go ahead and look because it's the only one I have and I'm proud of it.

I no longer felt that I didn't measure up to others, to my sister. By exposing my form, I was also allowing the inner me to be revealed in a more open and authentic way. It turned out to be less painful to show myself than to keep myself under lock and key.

But I have taken a giant step backward. Without the most obvious of my feminine attributes, I once again feel less-than. I want to hide, to fold in on myself, to keep everyone at bay. Having breast cancer assaulted a large part of my identity and was crushing me. What once made me feel womanly was now just a garish scar, red and erratic, raw and glaring. And if I am honest with myself, I once again feel inferior to Cindy.

I have gone from the swimsuit issue to taking issue with my swimsuit. From pretend falsies to real ones. From losing my sex appeal to appealing my loss. From a two-piece to a no-piece; I will not be putting a swimsuit on this year.

I have been robbed of the joy of embracing the beach, falling into the luxury of leaving my cares behind and taking those first strides across the sand, feeling at home because that is what Rehoboth is to me.

I hear Cindy's car pull into the driveway. Big hugs and smiles abound as I help tote her stuff into the house. I grab a pink-handled bag from the front seat, but she gently takes it from me.

"I've got this. How about you take my carryall with the beach towels and lotion?"

Dinner is a feast of old times: girl talk, laughter, gossip, and gratitude. Once the dishes are cleared, she grabs the wine glasses from the table and I carry over the remaining bottle of wine. We each nestle into a corner of the comfortable, flowered couch and put our bare feet up on the nicked and weathered coffee table. Eventually, the talk turns to a loose itinerary for the next day, our first together since last summer.

"How about an early morning stroll along the boardwalk?" Cindy offers up. "Then we can come back to the house and get ready for the—"

I put up my hand to stop her. A cross-breeze blows through the open kitchen window. Voices float down from the upper deck next door. I take another pull of my drink, the etched pelican on the glass appearing red from the liquid behind it.

"That sounds good, but remember I told you I would not be bringing a swimsuit?"

She takes in this decree and nods her head. But being who she is, she cannot help but urge me to get back to normal. After all, wasn't it her encouragement that got me through my physical recuperation? Now I need to address my emotional recovery, she says.

Cindy continued, "You have been my idol, you know. You have a strength and courage I wish I had. I don't mean to pressure you. It's just that this time in Rehoboth is what sustains both of us all year long. I'm afraid if we let it slip by, you will stay stuck in a rut. By all means, be angry about what you've been through, but let me help you fight against your despair." She sets her glass on the coffee table.

I know my sister well. I catch a slight glimmer in her eye that tells me she has something up her sleeve. I let out a sigh.

She gets up and goes to the small, pink bag that sits at the bottom of the steps leading up to our childhood bedrooms. "Here," she says, and holds out the bundle.

"What's this? A bra from Victoria's Secret?" I didn't mean for it to come out snotty. I make no move to take the object from her, although her gesture is touching. I swirl the remaining ounce of Shiraz, which reflects back to my internal miasma.

"I knew you could not bring yourself to try on any mastectomy swimsuits, so I bought one for you. I honestly think it will be very pretty on you." She is still standing above me, the tissue paper inside crinkling as she sets the bag on the table. She sits back down on the edge of the sofa, the soft lamplight highlighting the flecks of gold in her compassionate eyes.

I wade through the tissue paper to find a pink one-piece, sprinkled with stars, the bust filled with two silicone inserts. "Thank you, Cindy, but I honestly don't think I'm ready."

"Sleep on it, ok?"

"Will do."

And with that, we say good night.

The next morning, the warm smells of French toast and bacon waft up the stairs and tickle me awake. I run a comb through my hair and skip down to the kitchen in my pj's, which consist of a T-shirt and boxer shorts. Cindy is also in pj's, an ensemble with starfish on them. She is busy at the stove, flipping the slices of the egg-coated bread.

With steaming cups of coffee, we sit down to eat and I find I am famished.

"So, what do you say about going to the beach?" Cindy ventures, sticking another syrupy forkful into her mouth.

"You are a hard sell, woman, do you know that?" I laugh. "I will try the suit on, but that's it."

"That's all I ask. I'll clean up while you go get changed."

I come down with my cover-up over the suit. Cindy gives me a smirk, so I shed the top layer.

"Wow, you look so good! What do you think?"

I shrugged and offer, "Not bad. Better than I thought."

"Wait!" Cindy exclaims. "I forgot the most important thing. Now where did I put it?" She makes a show of looking around the room, peering under a magazine on an end table, and then rooting through her carryall while pushing aside the towels. "Here it is!"

I look, but see nothing. She holds her empty hands about six inches apart and raises them to her face.

"Ladies and gentlemen, be the first to witness—click—the comeback of the famous "Babette!"—click. After years in hiding—click—she once again emerges onto the modeling scene—click—taking her rightful place as the most beautiful woman in the world!"

"Noooo, stop!" I sputter as I run to hide behind the couch.

"Click, click, click." Cindy is kneeling beside me, furiously snapping her air camera.

I jump up and run into the kitchen, but she follows me.

"Still a raging beauty—click. How does she do it, folks? Click."

"Ok, ok . . . you win! I'll wear the darn swimsuit to the beach. Give me that thing." I grab the air camera and start shooting her. "Click. Ladies and gentlemen, the most annoying—click—sister—click—in the world! Click. She won't leave Babette alone to fade into obscurity! Click."

Cindy sticks out her tongue.

A tear leaves a trail on my cheek. "She has a knack of knowing—click—just what to say and do—click—to support her stubborn sister. Click."

We fall into each other's arms amidst laughter and memories.

I am at the waterline. The surf swirls around my ankles. The sun caresses my soul. I want to live in the moment—this moment—to just be and believe that everything will be ok. The sun will rise and set, the ocean will acquiesce its tides to the moon, new sand will be born from crumbling mountains, and I will breathe and let go, inhale and release, be filled through emptiness.

In the midst of this coveted serenity, a thought suddenly occurs. I can't help but laugh out loud when the words come. Rehoboth, Cindy, and I . . . we're . . . well-suited.

CHRIS JACOBSEN IS WELL ACQUAINTED WITH THE ANGST THAT GOES ALONG WITH TRYING ON SWIMSUITS PRIOR TO THE START OF SUMMER. HAVING SEVERAL (TOO MANY) CLOSE FRIENDS DEAL WITH SURGERY DUE TO BREAST CANCER MADE CHRIS CONSIDER HOW MUCH MORE DIFFICULT IT WOULD BE, UNDER THAT CIRCUMSTANCE, TO FACE THE MIRROR. "THE SWIMSUIT ISSUE" IS CHRIS'S SECOND STORY TO BE PUBLISHED IN ONE OF THE REHOBOTH BEACH READS BOOKS. THE FIRST ONE, "THE GREAT REHOBOTH RACE," WAS INCLUDED IN *THE BOARDWALK*. CHRIS WOULD LOVE TO KNOW HOW MANY READERS, UPON COMPLETION OF THE STORY, GOOGLED THE 1964 *SPORTS ILLUSTRATED* SWIMSUIT ISSUE TO CHECK OUT THE REAL BABETTE!

JUDGE'S COMMENT

"The Swimsuit Issue" is a brave story, exploring the relationships between sisters and recovery from a most intimate loss. Past memories of Rehoboth Beach gain restorative and healing powers in the present-day trauma of breast cancer. A sensitive subject, well handled.

A Beautifully Disturbing Day at the Beach

By John Edmonds

What a fantastic summer day, Simon thought as he scanned the beach. His senses were inundated with the familiar beach aromas of sunscreen and salty air, combined with the sounds of the surf, the chatter of beachgoers, and the laughter of children. These smells and sounds meant "vacation" to Simon. He was flooded with memories of past summer vacations with his parents to this very beach.

He had been looking forward to this week since his vacation a year ago. Simon was camped out on the same spot, on the same beach as he was last year. In fact, he was wearing the same bathing suit, and using the same towel, same umbrella, and same bottle of sunscreen as last year. As he looked around, he noticed nothing had really changed at the beach, either. He saw the same Dolles, same Candy Kitchen, and same Funland on the boardwalk. Simon was not a fan of change, so all of this was just fine with him.

Lying on his beach towel close to the surf, Simon heard another familiar sound—the unmistakable distant hum of an airplane engine. Leaning up on his elbows and scanning the sky, he discovered its source. The familiar yellow plane, pulling a long banner, lumbered into view as it headed north along the crowded beach. He had always been amazed at how the planes appeared to be moving so slowly, but somehow avoided falling from the sky. The towed banner displayed the locally well-known logo of Grotto Pizza, and Simon decided then and there he would visit the restaurant for dinner.

Simon's mental vision of biting into cheesy pizza goodness was interrupted by a not-so-familiar sound. The sound of a misfiring engine brought his attention back to the airplane. Clouds of dark smoke began trailing the plane, as it was obviously having engine trouble. The sputtering of the engine continued, as did the smoke, for a few more seconds and then . . . silence.

Simon watched in horror as the plane quickly lost altitude and plummeted toward the choppy ocean below. The plane fell from the sky and hit the water, causing an enormous splash that he could only compare to those he had seen of exploding shells in naval warfare movies. As he stared, frozen with shock, the banner slowly floated to the water's surface.

Simon jumped to his feet. His trance broken, he instinctively moved toward the water to get a better view of the crashed plane. It was about two hundred yards offshore, and only the top of the yellow wings and tail were visible, as a reminder that the plane had sunk below the surface. There was no sign of the pilot.

It suddenly dawned on Simon that he was the only person on the beach who seemed interested in the crashed plane. In fact, he was the only one even looking in the plane's direction. He turned to a young couple with their child near the water's edge.

"Did you see that plane go down?"

The young woman looked at her husband and then back at Simon. She gathered her child, and the three of them moved away with puzzled looks on their faces. Simon scanned the waterline of the beach and noticed that no one seemed aware of what had just happened.

Even the lifeguards just sat in their chairs, oblivious to the events unfolding. *How could that be?*

Simon realized that precious time was slipping away for the pilot, if he had survived the crash. With his mind racing, Simon ran to the surf and plunged into the water, swimming toward the plane. He was a strong swimmer, thanks to his years working summers as a lifeguard during high school and college. He swam at a steady pace, so as not to tire too soon, and reached the plane in what seemed like an eternity, yet in reality, it took only about five minutes.

To his relief, the plane was still floating, though he didn't know for how long. Pausing to catch his breath, Simon held on to the wing's edge, trying to gather his thoughts. The cockpit was underwater, and still no sign of the pilot. After scanning the wreck site, and seeing no boats approaching to assist, Simon moved closer to the fuselage of the plane. Taking a deep breath, he dove.

Visibility was poor in the murky water, and he depended on touch to reach the cockpit door. Finding the handle, Simon turned and pulled. The door wouldn't budge. He surfaced for a breath and returned to the door, this time placing his feet on either side for leverage. The door stubbornly gave way, and Simon surfaced for another breath. Regaining his composure and additional oxygen, he dove a third time and cautiously swam into the cockpit. Using his outstretched arms, Simon reached from one end of the cockpit to the other, but found nothing but debris.

Confused and needing air, Simon suddenly felt the plane shift and shudder. Peeking out the cockpit window toward the surface, he realized that the light reflecting from the surface was dimming. The plane was sinking—with him in it. He dove out the door and kicked to the surface. Simon gazed down at the plane as he swam upward. The yellow blur soon disappeared into the dark depths of the Atlantic.

As he broke the surface of the water, Simon quickly exhaled and sucked in precious air. He floated for several minutes to rest until his breathing returned to normal. The exhaustion he felt was replaced by disappointment that he had been unable to save the pilot. He was also confused about what had happened. The cockpit doors were sealed, and there was no sign of anyone inside.

Simon's attention turned to getting back to shore and reporting his findings. He looked in the direction where he thought he should see the beach, but all he could see was a thick, gray fogbank, running north and south and obscuring any view of land. *Where did that come from?* Turning and looking out to the open sea, Simon observed clear skies and the distant horizon. There was no sign of any weather disturbance. Fear crept into Simon's psyche. Up to now, adrenaline had controlled his emotions. *What have I gotten myself into,* he thought, as he started to swim toward where he thought the beach should be.

It took him only a few minutes to reach the edge of the fog. Simon's anxiety ratcheted up a notch as he entered the mist. Fearful of being disoriented, he picked up his pace and concentrated on keeping on a straight line toward shore. The water seemed to calm as the fog enveloped him, but more disturbing was the sudden drop in water temperature. Simon was familiar with swimming through currents of different temperatures, but this was a drastic change—a twenty- to thirty-degree drop. As a shiver shook his body, he fought to control the panic.

Simon continued to stroke and kick at an even pace, his survival instincts kicking in. The cold was draining what little energy he had left. When he dared to open his eyes, he saw nothing but the fog and imagined it choking him.

Then he heard the surf, and a surge of relief warmed him briefly. But Simon soon felt the swells of the waves pull his body. It was becoming harder and harder for him to lift his arms and kick his legs to maintain forward momentum. He was cold to the point of numbness as hypothermia seized his body. Perplexing, disjointed thoughts flooded his mind. *I must reach shore, or I'm going to die,* his mind's voice was shouting, but it sounded distant.

Tumbling, tumbling, Simon felt his body being tossed around like a rag doll until he was pounded to the sandy bottom of the beach. He crawled through the wet sand with the last of his strength to distance himself from the waves. When Simon believed he was beyond the reach of the undertow, he collapsed onto the sand.

Not sure how long he had lain in this spot, Simon raised himself with his arms and lifted his head. At first, he thought hypothermia was still playing tricks. In front of him, the boardwalk lay in ruins, reduced to scrambled piles of broken boards and pilings. Debris littered the beach. The buildings that housed Dolles, Candy Kitchen, Funland, and everything in-between were unrecognizable. There was destruction as far as the eye could see. He shook his head and closed his eyes, hoping that when he reopened them, everything would return to normal. It didn't.

Then, from a distance, Simon saw a lone figure walking in his direction from what used to be the boardwalk. Still lacking the strength to stand, he waited for the person to approach. It was a fireman, dressed in full firefighting attire, including boots and helmet.

"What in the hell are you doing out here?" the fireman asked, as he knelt in front of Simon.

Simon opened his mouth to respond, but the words would not come out.

"And what the hell are you doing swimming in the ocean in March? That water is cold enough to kill you in short order."

Again, Simon tried to respond, but with the same result.

"Not to mention picking the day after the worst Nor'easter to hit this area in a long time. They're calling it 'the storm of the century.' Yeah, they'll be looking back on 1962 for a long, long time. You need some help?"

March? . . . Storm? . . . 1962? . . . what is he talking about? Simon's head was spinning and exhaustion overcame him. He fainted onto the sand.

"Sir? Excuse me, Sir."

The voice sounded distant to Simon, but he sensed urgency in the tone and attempted to open his eyes.

"Sir, you should move your stuff, or it's going to get soaked. The tide's coming in."

Simon felt the wet, cold sensation of water lapping at his feet.

"I know what that's like," continued the voice. "I've fallen asleep on the beach and had all my gear ruined, including my cell phone."

Simon opened his eyes to find the same crowded beach he had left when he attempted to save the pilot of the downed plane.

"Not to mention a massive sunburn, which, by the way, you're going to have."

Simon slowly rose to his feet as a wave spilled up over the end of his towel. He quickly lifted the backpack with his phone and wallet. He turned to the young man who had spoken to him.

"I really appreciate you telling me before my stuff got wet," he said to the man. Simon looked around. Dolles, Candy Kitchen, and Funland were all bustling with throngs of beachgoers.

"No problem," the man said as he turned and walked away.

Wow, Simon thought. *That was some dream.* Simon gathered his things and moved them farther back on the beach. He took a deep breath and headed in the direction of the water to cool off. He wasn't going to let a weird dream ruin what was left of a great beach day.

Simon waded into the cool surf. He bent over and splashed water on his arms and upper body. He felt the tension melt away and decided to put the crazy dream out of his mind.

As Simon turned to return to his towel, something caught his eye in the surf. At first, he thought it was a boogie board that had been lost.

But as the waves brought it closer to him, he saw that it was not a boogie board, but rather a square, faded, orange cushion—the kind of seat cushion that doubles as a floating device. Simon grabbed it before the undertow could take it back. He turned it over and stenciled on the back in black letters were the words:

DELAWARE AERIAL ADVERTISING

Simon started to scream.

JOHN EDMONDS IS A SIXTEEN-YEAR RESIDENT OF REHOBOTH BEACH WITH HIS WIFE, LISA. SINCE HE CAN REMEMBER, JOHN HAS ALWAYS HAD A PASSION FOR READING, WHICH HAS INSPIRED HIM LATER IN LIFE TO BECOME A STORYTELLER AND AUTHOR NUMEROUS SHORT STORIES. JOHN IS VERY EXCITED TO HAVE HIS FIRST PUBLISHED WORK IN *BEACH LIFE*. HE AND LISA, WHO IS A LOCAL ARTIST, CURRENTLY SPEND MOST OF THEIR TIME AT CAPE TREASURE, THEIR COASTAL HOME DÉCOR AND GIFT STORE IN MILTON, AND AT HOME WITH THEIR THREE RESCUE "PUPPIES." MUCH OF JOHN'S WRITING IS INSPIRED BY THE LOCAL DELAWARE BEACHES AND THE LIFETIME OF MEMORIES THEY HAVE PROVIDED. JOHN IS CURRENTLY WORKING ON HIS FIRST NOVEL, WHICH HE HOPES WILL SOMEDAY BE PUBLISHED.

Rearrangements

By Marie Lathers

I'm Evelyn Brine, and it's good to meet you. Is this your first time in Rehoboth? No? Well, then, maybe you've seen one of my arrangements. I start with a large scallop shell, and then I put smaller treasures in it—a whelk, a shark's eye, a piece of sea glass—the kinds of things you find on the beach here. Let's just say that the owners of good restaurants in town know what it means to provide a beach-worthy centerpiece on every table. My arrangements distinguish the Rehoboth eateries from the ones in Dewey and Bethany. And they pay me seven dollars a centerpiece, which sure adds up! You won't catch me wondering where my money went at the end of my life—it's in the bank. What I haven't spent on long-distance calls, that is, because of my granddaughter Penny.

Penny used to run my phone bills out of sight. She has one of those iPhones now, so long distance is the same as local, but she hardly even talks on the phone anymore. She works over at City Hall, designing pamphlets for the tourists. Insists on living here with me, in my old place. I'm a lucky grandmother, that's for sure. We get along just fine. But it took a while for us to get there. It's the summer of 2013, so that makes it two years since the thaw.

"Penny, I'm too old for this," I told her when she started her complaining about everything—every sound I made, every meal I cooked, every place I put a knickknack—in my *own home.* "You're living in my place, and I've a right to exist in it just like I always have, without a young upstart coming back from a fancy college and bossing me around." I paused, for effect. "And that's the first and last time I'm going to remind you of that."

I was seventy-four years old and happy enough with my life the way it was. I didn't ask Penny's mother to send her here to Rehoboth from DC after she finished college with a C average, thirty thousand dollars in student loans, and a bad attitude. Great way to start off in life! But she did. My daughter sent her here lickety-split once she realized Penny had no more intention of pursuing a career in "interdisciplinary studies"—whatever that is—than she did in paying back her loans.

Four years she spent in that private college in the mountains of Virginia, long enough to perfect her taste for high-elevation life and her distaste for sea-level common sense. But when she was a child, oh, mighty, you couldn't keep her off the beach. Even promising an ice cream if she'd walk on up to the boardwalk couldn't get her to leave the sand and waves behind. That girl loved the ocean and everything in and around it. Until she went hormonal, that is. Adolescence has wrecked many a young girl who was otherwise on the road to a healthy and worthwhile life, and it left Penny in pieces.

At first, she resisted, like some do. "But I don't want to grow up!" she wailed at me that day in July when she woke up with cramps and knew her childhood was over. She was only twelve years old, poor thing—not even a teenager. The next summer, she did nothing but mope around as if Rehoboth were the dark side of the moon and she had been sent here to serve out a prison sentence. Back then, from the time Penny was school age, her mother sent the child to me for most of the summer while she ran around, looking for a new husband. And then another new one. Penny had other ideas. "I don't want to have to kiss boys. I don't want to have to be nice and pretty and wear makeup. I don't want to get married over and over!" Easy enough to see that she didn't want to be like her mother.

Penny's change coincided with Gerald's passing, and I spent a few years at my wits' end for want of something to occupy me. For so long, my time was devoted to taking him to doctors' appointments, driving back and forth between here and Beebe Hospital. Afterwards, the long hours stretched out before me with not much to fill them. Sometimes I even made the trip to the hospital in my car, ate at the cafeteria, and drove back home, just to fill the empty space of time. But then there was hormonal Penny, filling it with her complaints.

"I miss my friends!" she wailed, day after day. Talking on the phone for hours at a time with Ashley, Heather, and Lindsay about boys named Kyle, Shane, and Jordan wasn't good enough for her. "Lindsay's in New York City for the summer, and Heather's at a co-ed camp!"

She made no attempt to find the local boys attractive. I even arranged a date between her and Randall, Mr. Watson's grandson, which made her so mad she didn't talk to me for an entire morning.

"*Randall.* They don't even call him 'Randy,' and have you even seen his pimples? The hot beach sun can't even dry them out! He smells like a whelk shell that had a slimy animal inside," she announced after the date, which lasted all of twenty-three minutes and consisted of a walk on the boardwalk to the arcade.

I was pleased she at least remembered what a dead shell animal smelled like.

"I told him the Rehoboth arcade has nothing but old video games, and that everyone in DC is sick to death of Mortal Kombat!"

She finally met a fourteen-year-old hussified girl by the name of 'Zoe' whom she moped around with for two summers. Once, I smelled tobacco on her and threatened her with no telephone time at all if I smelled it again.

Once she was in high school, Penny insisted to her mother that she would not in any way, shape, or form agree to spend vacation with me in my "old home full of old things made for old people." But my daughter, just as stubborn and with another marriage on the rocks, needed somewhere to board Penny. She sent the girl off to a horse ranch in Virginia, which explains why Penny ended up at a college that was way too expensive and lacking in any major study area that might conceivably lead to a career.

So there she was one morning on my doorstep, three weeks after her college graduation, after I hadn't laid eyes on her for seven years. She had four suitcases and looked as if she'd been starving herself. Meanwhile, I discovered my passion one day at the diner, staring at the blank table in front of me and thinking how nice it would look with a centerpiece. No one likes a blank space. Gerald always said I had an eye for fashion, and he was right. My passion had been keeping me sane.

"Mom says she needs me out of the house for at least two months, or she and Darryl will end up in divorce court. Darryl couldn't deal with me. And by the way, I hope you have a decent TV now, because I watch the three big ones every afternoon—*All My Children, Days of Our Lives,* and *General Hospital*—and if I miss one single day, my sorority sisters will disown me."

Apparently, that so-called college had allowed her to sign up for only morning classes so she and her "sisters" could spend every afternoon on the soaps. They call that an education! She intended to spend the summer watching that junk while she talked on the phone with Erika, Courtney, and Whitney, who didn't seem to have found jobs, either.

"That's just fine with me," I told her, "since I spend every afternoon on the porch making my arrangements, which are on the tables of many restaurants in Rehoboth. Maybe you'll see one if you ever take your eyes off the TV long enough to go out to eat with me. Until then, you can sit in front of my very capable fifteen-year-old color TV that your grandpa bought me for Christmas, bless his soul."

That's where we stood after a month—Penny watching the soaps, and me attempting to make meals that would put some flesh back on her and working on my centerpieces—when I heard her scream and then wail like a child, wail like she did when she realized being a woman was not a ride in the park. She ran looking for me on the porch, which doubled as my shell studio, and then came wailing into the dining room.

"Cancelled! Grandma! They're threatening to cancel the soaps! What the hell will I *do?* I'll simply DIE!" She'd just gotten off the phone with Whitney, who had explained the situation to her. The second decade of the twenty-first century was headed for disaster, apparently.

I'd told Penny that cursing was not allowed in my home, but she must not have heard me. So I told her to take that wax out of her ears because I had none in mine, and I simply did not want to hear that kind of language. "And another thing," I added, "once those soaps are off the air, you'll have a reason to get out into the actual air—the air that the Lord meant for you to breathe. And maybe you'll get some exercise."

Well, she just kept right on moping and right on watching the soaps, even though their days were apparently numbered. And I kept right on making my arrangements on the porch, where I had card tables set up to hold shoeboxes full of the different categories of shells, and then different-sized boxes to put them in and drive them around town. My mornings were spent on the beach and my afternoons on my craft, which made for a good, wholesome, and healthy life if you ask me or anyone I know.

Then, lo and behold, one day Penny just walked on out onto the porch, sat down, and started sorting shells. She remembered the names and muttered them while she worked. She'd left the TV volume up loud, and someone was on trial for something on one of those crazy shows. After an hour, I went in and turned it off, and Penny didn't say a word. We sat like that until dinnertime, sorting shells and sea glass and making centerpieces. Then she said she was hungry. I made us egg salad sandwiches with chips, pickles, and lemonade, and we had the best time laughing and giggling over all kinds of whatnot.

Right before bedtime, Penny got serious. "It turns out they're only going to cancel *All My Children,* but I'm done with the soaps, Grandma." She paused. "Whitney's grandpa died last week and she stopped watching. I told her I'd stop, too." She looked at me and I looked back, and for the first time in forever, we really saw each other.

"I'm sorry for your friend, Penny. And you know, it sure would be nice to spend time together. I've missed your company."

We looked at each other again and smiled wide summer smiles.

"After all, these are the days of *our* lives."

MARIE LATHERS GREW UP IN SILVER SPRING, MD, AND SPENT MANY WONDERFUL SUMMER DAYS AT REHOBOTH BEACH. SHE TEACHES HUMANITIES AT CASE WESTERN RESERVE UNIVERSITY IN CLEVELAND, OH, AND HAS PUBLISHED ACADEMIC ARTICLES AND BOOKS ON LITERATURE, ART, AND FILM. HER SHORT STORIES AND CREATIVE ESSAYS HAVE BEEN PUBLISHED IN OUTLETS SUCH AS *SLOW TRAINS LITERARY JOURNAL, DEEP SOUTH MAGAZINE,* AND *BEWILDERING STORIES* (THE LATTER UNDER THE NAME MARIE CHAPMAN). SHE ALSO HAS AN ESSAY IN THE 2017 COLLECTION *SOAP OPERA CONFIDENTIAL,* PUBLISHED BY MCFARLAND. SHE IS WORKING ON A COMING-OF-AGE NOVEL SET IN WHEATON, MD, DURING THE WATERGATE YEARS.

JUDGE'S COMMENT

The voice and perspective of the main character hooked me immediately. It was an unusual way to tell a story, but it absolutely worked in this case—light enough for a beach read but strong enough to deliver the message home.

Some Girls

By Michael Sprouse

Hamilton's eyelids shot open as if he were being snapped back to consciousness by a county fair hypnotist. As he wiped sweat from his face with trembling hands, he realized he couldn't remember his dream, but whatever it had been, it had been bad enough that he had subconsciously forced himself out of it.

Ham blinked his eyes several times. Except for the slow, deep breaths he was using to calm himself, he remained motionless in bed. He needed to clear his mind.

Everything in his tiny bedroom seemed farther away than usual and tinged in a pale, bluish haze. A gauzy curtain swayed silently like a dancer's skirt, as an ocean-scented, Delaware nighttime breeze teased its way through his open window. The air felt cool against his flushed forehead, and the sensation gently ushered him back to reality.

He heard the unmistakable roar of a motorcycle speeding down the highway from what he thought must be several blocks away. It surprised him how far sound carried in the middle of the night. Someone was either headed to work very early or returning home very late. He wondered if anyone else was out there, also lying awake in the middle of the night, listening to the same sound. He couldn't decide whether the possibility was amazing or just lonely.

He turned his head to gaze at the slightly faded Polaroid occupying the Dollar Store frame that sat on his nightstand. It was a photo of a tiny baby, held cautiously by a man he didn't know.

The man was his father and namesake. His mother, Deannie, once told him that it was the only photograph of the two of them together. The man was handsome and young, grinning, and clearly happy, yet something about his expression revealed a kind of uneasiness. Perhaps, Ham thought, he had seen into the future. He was listed as MIA in '67 when Ham was only two.

Ham thought about the mysterious man in the photograph often. Occasionally, he created memories of events that never happened, centered around the father he didn't remember. The memories brought him comfort and made him feel safe, or at least made him believe, if only temporarily, that he was no different than every other kid he knew—kids with living fathers.

Ham's room had now taken on the soft, pinkish-orange glow that comes shortly before sunrise. He guessed that it was sometime between four and six thirty. The only thing Ham knew for certain was the date—June 21, 1978—the first day of summer and the morning of his thirteenth birthday.

Ham lay in bed for what felt like a very long time, gazing at the ceiling and contemplating his new age. Was it a milestone? Possibly. Probably. Was he supposed to feel different? *Did* he feel different? He wasn't certain.

Ham heard his mother shuffling through her usual morning routine before heading off to work as a day clerk at the Henlopen Hotel in Rehoboth Beach. Deannie supplemented her minimum-wage job tending bar and waitressing at a local bayside restaurant, but money was always tight.

The "extravagances," as she liked to call to them, were few and far between. "We're poor but happy, kiddo." Ham would smile in agreement each time she said this, which was frequently, but he would silently wonder about his mother's definition of happiness.

Their apartment was small and basic—two bedrooms, one bathroom, and a living room/dining room combo. It took up the top story of an old Victorian house on Savannah Road, a handful of blocks from Lewes Beach.

Ham rose from bed and shuffled into the kitchen.

"Good morning, Mom."

"Hey, birthday boy! How did you sleep?"

"Pretty good, I guess."

The mingled, pungent scents of coffee and Deannie's perfume filled the room. Ham opened the cabinet and pulled out a box of Kaboom cereal and a bowl.

"What? No Lucky Charms for a lucky birthday boy?" Deannie asked with a wink.

"Nah, not today, Mom. But you never know. If I just happen to find a pot o' gold today, I'll alert the press before we head to Mexico."

Ham filled the bowl with his favorite cereal as Deannie grabbed the milk from the fridge. She poured it over the cereal with a curtsy, her hand swirling away from her forehead as if she were serving a king.

"For your majesty on this grand and special occasion, kind sir," she said with a theatrical, hoity-toity British accent that made Ham laugh.

Deannie pulled a tube of lipstick from her purse, which was sitting on the counter. "Look, honey," she said, while applying the coral-red color to her lips. "I hate to do it, but I have to go to work soon. I wish I could play hooky and hang out with you on your birthday—but, well, you know how busy it is at the hotel this time of year."

Ham watched as Deannie blotted her lipstick on a paper napkin and then quickly glanced at her watch. He understood that she couldn't afford to be late.

"Anyway, I should be home around four. I was thinking, maybe we could go into Rehoboth and go bowling tonight. Wouldn't that be fun?"

Ham realized that the cost of the game, the two beers Deannie would probably drink, plus the cost of the cheeseburgers they'd have for dinner would make it a pretty pricey outing. He loved the idea, but not if it was going to put a dent in her wallet, so he decided not to seem too excited.

"Yeah, Mom. Sounds fine."

"Oh? You don't sound thrilled by the idea."

"No, really. That sounds great. I'm just . . . well, can we afford to do that?"

"Oh, now, don't you worry about that, sweetie. It's all fine. It's your birthday, for chrissake! Sometimes, kiddo, you just gotta splurge a little bit. Maybe we can grab some ice cream after on the boardwalk. We'll live it up! Park ourselves on a bench, people watch, stare at the ocean. *That* will be fun, won't it? I love you so much, kiddo." Deannie planted a kiss on Ham's cheek and headed out the door.

As she started down the stairwell, Deannie shouted, "Have a good time today—do something *fun!* And don't forget to lock up. God—what a beautiful morning!"

"Thanks, Mom. Love you, too," Ham shouted back.

He listened as his mother's footsteps descended the wooden staircase. A minute later, he heard the door shut on their 1967 Rambler, and the low, stubborn rumble of the engine as the car churned to a start, followed by the occasional echo of backfire as she headed down Savannah Road.

As Ham swallowed the final bite of bear-, lion-, and star-shaped marshmallows, three quick thoughts formed in his head: he was probably too old for Kaboom now, he had to wash his mother's lipstick off his face, and he was going to spend the day at the beach.

Ham placed the bowl and spoon in the sink and then walked to the Magnavox AM/FM stereo console that took up a large portion of the living room. The massive music machine, which came with the apartment, had sat in the same spot for as many years as he could remember.

Ham's favorite part was the turntable. Between Deannie's records from her younger days and the albums that Ham had managed to purchase with money from odd jobs around the neighborhood, they had built a decent collection of music.

He took meticulous care of the albums, keeping them free from lint, dust, and scratches. He selected *Aja* by Steely Dan from the collection that he had alphabetized earlier in the week. Ham started humming along to "Black Cow" as he thought about his plan to get to the boardwalk. He hitchhiked on occasion, but this time, he thought, he would ride his bike.

He had made the flat, roughly eight-mile journey countless times. He liked the sweet, summer-infused scent of the farmland that bordered most of the trek along the Coastal Highway from Lewes to Rehoboth. It would be an easy ride and he enjoyed the solitude.

After his shower, Ham got dressed. He threw on a pair of cut-off jeans, his well-worn Adidas tennis shoes, and his favorite T-shirt.

Just as he was about to turn off the stereo and head out the door, a thought popped into his head. He had half a joint hidden under the base of the lava lamp in his room. An older friend had given it to him on the last day of school.

He had only smoked pot a few times, but he enjoyed the feeling. His friend had called getting stoned in the morning "wake and bake," which Ham thought was hilarious. He had never smoked pot by himself, and certainly not this early in the day, but it was his *birthday* after all, for chrissake. Plus, it was the first day of summer. He stepped back into his room, lifted the lamp, and grabbed the joint.

Ham walked back to the stereo console and turned off the turntable. He carefully removed the album and placed it in its proper spot before turning on the FM radio.

He kept the dial set to a Philadelphia-based progressive rock station that would fade in and out, depending on the weather. The DJ's mellow voice was praising a concert that he had seen the night before in some club on South Street.

Ham grabbed a box of wooden matches from the kitchen counter and, leaving the door open, stepped outside onto the small landing at the top of the stairs. He held the joint tightly between his index finger and thumb, brought it to his lips, and lit it. He inhaled deeply, holding the smoke in his lungs for a moment before releasing.

After the second hit, Ham started to sense the buzz. He now noticed—with *far* more intensity than before—that it was an absolutely, incredibly beautiful morning. The trees lazily swayed back and forth with the June breeze. There seemed to be an entire orchestra of birdsong, as robins skittered from branch to branch. The sky was sharply clear and wildly blue. The spicy scent of freshly cut grass mingled with sweet-smelling lilac. The morning sun sparkled on every surface. He was now most definitely stoned and all the happier for it. Ham closed his eyes and took a long, relaxing, deep breath, taking in as much of the moment as possible.

Suddenly, Mick Jagger's distinctive voice came blasting out of the stereo. It was the single "Shattered" off the latest Stones' album *Some Girls*. Though he wasn't really expecting one, and he hadn't mentioned it to Deannie, the album was the only birthday gift he truly wanted. He had already heard several of the tracks on the radio and he liked each one, but the song that really had him was "Shattered." The Jagger hook was potent.

He longed for the album. It was new and incredibly popular, which meant that finding *Some Girls* wasn't easy. Whenever he did see a copy in the record store, he didn't have enough cash on him to make the purchase. It was a common situation for Ham.

Though he had managed to save *some* money for his birthday, he was still roughly three dollars short the cost of *Some Girls*. He forced the thought out of his mind. "Screw it," he said aloud. He was going to the boardwalk, and he was going to have as much fun as $5.77 would allow.

The sun was hot during his ride down the Coastal Highway. Once he finally made his way to Rehoboth Avenue, Ham felt the heat on his neck and arms. It was one of his favorite things about summer. He loved the way his slightly sunburned skin tingled in the cool, ocean breeze.

When he reached the boardwalk, Ham locked up his bike, veered through the crowd, and headed to Funland. Even though he couldn't afford his favorite album, he could play a hell of a lot of Space Invaders and pinball with the cash in his pocket and still have enough left over for Thrasher fries and a Dr. Pepper.

Funland was swelteringly hot and packed full of flush-faced kids darting in every direction while overheated, frustrated parents with their hands full of tokens and tickets tried to keep them under control. Strings of fluorescent, stuffed animals with large, googly, plastic eyes swayed from the top of every booth. He was still a little stoned, and the experience felt like a swirling mass of colors, blinking lights, ringing bells, laughter, and shrieks.

Ham exchanged two of his dollars for tokens and parked himself in front of the Space Invaders machine. After close to an hour lost in a pulsating world of alien invasion, defending the earth from little green men, he was dripping with sweat and his hand was beginning to cramp.

Ham stepped back from the machine, and he began to shake the stiffness out of his hand. His eyes were watering, and his vision was slightly blurry from the marathon Space Invaders session.

Suddenly, the aroma of hot, boardwalk fries doused with vinegar wafted across his face in a breeze. It snapped him out of his sensory overload, and he realized he was famished. Making his way through the crowd of frantic kids, he headed to Thrashers.

Grabbing his medium-sized order of fries in one hand and a large Dr. Pepper in the other, he parked himself on the nearest empty bench. This was perfection. After he finished the last of his favorite boardwalk lunch, he kicked off his shoes, laced his fingers behind his head, closed his eyes, and basked in the early-afternoon sun.

For the second time that day, he heard the unmistakable sound of Mick Jagger's voice. A young, bronzed blonde, glistening with coconut-scented suntan oil, whizzed past the bench on skates, blasting "Shattered" from a huge boom box, just as an unusually strong gust of wind barreled down the boardwalk. Ham opened his eyes.

Something struck the side of his foot.

He looked down and saw that a faded, green ice cream wrapper had slapped up against his left ankle and heel in the breeze. As it started to blow off, he realized it was a twenty-dollar bill. Instantly and instinctively, he clamped his foot down, catching the edge of the bill. He gazed in amazement as the face of Andrew Jackson flapped across the top of his foot like a kite searching for wind. In one fell swoop, he reached down, grabbed the bill, and quickly shoved it in his pocket.

Ham sat motionless for a moment as he tried to quickly gather his thoughts. He glanced around in both directions as calmly as possible. No one was running at him screaming, "That's my twenty!" No child was crying and pointing in his direction. No one was holding an open wallet or rummaging through a purse. No one, in fact, looked as if they had lost anything at all.

He couldn't believe his luck. *I've got a freakin' twenty-dollar bill!* He had never had that much money on him at one time.

He felt like a rock star. He felt like Mick Jagger.

He abruptly remembered that a local church would sometimes scatter the boardwalk with relatively realistic twenties printed with a picture of an angry Jesus and scare stories on the back in a desperate attempt to draw the repentant into their fold. All it did, he thought, was piss off the sinners.

Ham carefully pulled the twenty from his pocket and examined the front and the back of the bill. It looked authentic. A mental list of everything he was going to buy that afternoon formed in his head. *Some Girls* was at the top.

A pang of guilt sparked in Ham's mind, eradicating his wish list like a wave hitting a sandcastle.

I should give the twenty to Mom. She works her ass off at that freakin' hotel, and she still doesn't make crap. Twenty bucks is a lot of money. Hell, I bet she doesn't even make twenty dollars in a whole day. It's the right thing to do. The mature thing.

The inner little boy—who still liked Kaboom for breakfast—regained control of the wheel. No. What I need to do is buy *Some Girls*. It's my birthday and I deserve it. Hell, the twenty landed on my foot for a reason. Jesus Christ. If not for that, then why else? I'll just buy the album, and maybe a couple of those cool T-shirts.

As Ham unlocked his bike, he was still amazed at how perfect the day had been so far and astonished by the twenty-dollar bill in his pocket. In just a few minutes, *Some Girls* would be his.

It was nearly five when Ham returned to the apartment and found Deannie waiting for him. She smiled and gestured at the small dining room table, where a large cupcake, thick with chocolate frosting and coated with purple sprinkles, sat on a plate. A slightly crooked, unlit, green candle protruded from the top.

"There he is! The birthday boy! You have a good time today, kiddo?"

"Yeah, Mom. It was great. What's this?" Ham feigned surprise. The birthday cupcake had long been the standard for both he and Deannie over the years.

"What do you *think* it is, Sherlock?" Deannie asked with a laugh. "It's your birthday cupcake! Now come sit over here and make a wish."

Ham took a seat next to his mother. He didn't believe in wishes. They rarely, if ever, came true. Deannie lit the candle and slid the plate with the cupcake in front of him. He closed his eyes, cleared his mind, and blew out the flame.

"What did you wish for?"

"Nothing, Mom."

"Hmm," she said, with a humorous lift of the eyebrow. "Was it, maybe, *this?*" Deannie pulled a thin, square-shaped gift from under the table. It was wrapped in the previous week's Sunday comics.

"Really? What's this?" Ham wasn't used to getting actual birthday gifts. Birthdays were usually celebrated with a movie or special treats.

"Just open it, kiddo."

He knew from the shape it was a record album. He ripped off the paper.

Some Girls.

"Mom. I . . . I don't know what to say."

"Well, the standard response is usually 'thank you,' " Deannie said with a little smirk. "I know you love The Stones. I mean, who doesn't, right? You're always turning up the volume when they play on the stereo. Anyway, one of the gals I work with, her boyfriend—real nice guy—works at the record store. I asked her if maybe he could hold the new Stones album for me when it came in. He even gave me a discount. I hope you like it, honey."

"Oh, Mom . . . you have no idea. I love it. Thank you so much." Ham smiled awkwardly.

"What is it?"

"Mom?"

"Yes, sweetie?"

"I have something for you, too."

"Honey, it's *your* birthday, not mine," Deannie said with a wink.

"It's just something I found at the beach."

"Did you find me some sea glass?"

Ham smiled shyly and held out his closed hand. His fingers trembled as he slowly opened them. The twenty-dollar bill unfurled in his palm like a leaf welcoming the spring.

"What's this? For me?"

"Like you say, Mom, 'Sometimes, you just gotta splurge a little.' "

In all his thirteen years, until that very moment, Ham had never seen his mother cry.

MICHAEL SPROUSE HAS BEEN WORKING PROFESSIONALLY IN THE ARTS FOR MORE THAN TWENTY-FIVE YEARS. HE IS ALSO AN AWARD-WINNING VISUAL ARTIST, ACCOMPLISHED MULTIMEDIA AND PRINT JOURNALIST, PHOTOGRAPHER, DIGITAL DESIGNER, AND THEATRICAL AND STAGE PROFESSIONAL. BEFORE MOVING TO THE DELAWARE SHORE IN 2002, HE WAS THE CO-OWNER AND CURATOR OF EKLEKTIKOS GALLERY OF CONTEMPORARY ART IN WASHINGTON, DC FOR ELEVEN YEARS. ADDITIONALLY, MICHAEL IS A CO-FOUNDER OF TWINFIN MEDIA AND THE ON-AIR HOST AND EXECUTIVE PRODUCER OF BOTH COASTAL CUISINE AND THE ARTS & ENTERTAINMENT REPORT, WHICH HAVE BEEN BROADCAST WEEKLY ON WRDE NBC COAST TV SINCE 2014.

"SOME GIRLS" IS LOOSELY BASED ON REAL PEOPLE AND ACTUAL EVENTS FROM HIS OWN PAST THAT OCCURRED IN THE SPRING AND SUMMER OF 1978 WHEN HE, TOO, CELEBRATED HIS THIRTEENTH BIRTHDAY, COLLECTED VINYL, AND WAS SLIGHTLY OBSESSED WITH THE ROLLING STONES.

JUDGES' COMMENTS

This story was a unique take on the standard beach read and offered a memorable character and storyline. A beach setting, combined with a vintage time period, along with the timelessness of tender relationships, make "Some Girls" an easy story to fall in love with. I liked the way this story built suspense, then sustained it (believably) till the last line. I also enjoyed the main character's point of view—a boy's sense of time, a day spent at his pace. This story about an adolescent son and his single mom is the antidote to every horror story about teen-parent interactions, by presenting a truly supportive parent whose faith in her son is rewarded when he returns the favor by supporting her: an uplifting, engaging tale. "Some Girls" is in some ways similar to O'Henry's "Gift of the Magi"—it has a moral story to tell about giving. It's a good-feeling story about relationships and their importance. A great beach read.

The Nereid's Wedding

By Elizabeth Michaelson Monaghan

Amy and Joe's Wedding Weekend Schedule
Wednesday, October 27, 3 p.m.
Bridal party's final fitting at Amy's parents' house.

Amy gazed at herself in the full-length mirror, adjusted her headpiece, and sighed. "I'm having second thoughts," she admitted.

"About the wedding?" I glanced at fellow bridesmaid Cat, horrified. Amy's wedding was in three days.

"No! About *this*." *This* was a thin circle of wire, covered in delicate, green glass beads: Amy's seaweed crown. "Why did I decide to wear a costume to my small, casual wedding?"

"Because you love the Sea Witch Festival?" I bent down to fluff out her train. "Because when Joe asked you to marry him, you said, 'Let's get married during the festival, and we can wear costumes'?"

Amy frowned. "I said that, didn't I?"

"You told Joe he would look great as a pirate," Cat chimed in. "You bought him a stuffed parrot on a strap to wear on his shoulder."

"Which he refused to do," Amy said.

"Luckily." I exchanged a look with Cat.

"So Joe's going to be a normal groom," said Amy, "but he'll be marrying a bride in a sea witch costume."

"A beautiful bride," I pointed out. "You look fantastic!"

It was true; Amy looked magnificent. Her tall, slim figure, usually hidden under her carpenter's uniform of multi-pocketed trousers and loose T-shirts, was suited to the dress's drama.

It started off tamely enough: pale-blue Dupioni silk, with a boat neck and fitted, three-quarter-length sleeves. But the bodice was embroidered with seahorses and starfish in a sky-blue thread, and Amy's ball-gown skirt was made of billowing layers of tiered organza. With her ruffled chapel-length train, the tail of which had been dip-dyed the blue-green color of the nearby ocean, it looked as if Amy were emerging from foam-topped waves. She made a glamorous, but undeniably exotic, bride—our very own Rehoboth Beach Sea Witch.

The headpiece—Amy's "seaweed" crown, custom made by an accessories designer she'd found on Etsy—*did* look a bit out of place on Amy's thick, straight blonde hair, though.

"Let's do your hair." Cat rummaged through her bag. She was in charge of wedding hair and makeup. "The half updo will give you a lot of volume, which will complement the dress."

Amy shot Cat a grateful look. "I love this dress," she said. "And the crown! I just doubt my ability to pull it off."

"I don't." Cat dug several bottles and a curling iron out of the bag. "Just be sure to avoid any open flames," she advised, as she aimed a can of hairspray at Amy.

When she was done, Amy's normally stick-straight hair was a mass of tousled, beachy curls. Two loose fishtail braids pinned to the back of her head kept her hair off her face. The effect was Bohemian and very pretty. I gingerly placed the crown on her head.

Cat and I cocked our heads thoughtfully. On the one hand, it *did* kind of look like Amy's head was draped in seaweed. On the other hand, the crown was undoubtedly elegant and flattering.

Amy's eyes met mine in the mirror and she grinned. "I love it."

Thursday, October 28: Amy and Cat's makeup trial. Sam bakes cake.

I was expecting an important call, so when it rang, I lunged without even checking the caller ID. I promptly tripped and landed facedown on the stone-tiled kitchen floor. *Ouch.*

"Samantha Collis," I gasped.

"I just ran into Don Runson," my mother announced. "He's getting married." There was a note of accusation in her voice.

I sat up and tentatively touched my forehead and brow bone. *Yow.* "That's nice."

"Samantha, why didn't you ever go on a second date with him? He's very good looking, *and* he's a dentist."

"Mom, he suggested I get braces and told me if I whitened my teeth, he'd take me to Ocean City for the weekend."

"Ocean City!" she hissed. "Well, no great loss, then." Apparently, the idea of visiting a rival resort town was more offensive than the insult. "How's Amy's wedding cake?"

"It's coming along." Amy and Joe's three-tiered wedding cake would consist of six-, eight-, and ten-inch round gingerbread cakes, filled and frosted with buttercream. I headed to the stove, wincing. The cakes had cooled on wire racks, but the kitchen still smelled sweetly of spices. I examined each cake: no burnt edges, no sunken centers. "I'm working on it now."

I briefly iced my throbbing eye, then got back to work, using a serrated knife to carefully level the top of each cake. I sliced each one into three even layers and stuck a ten-inch cake round to a cardboard circle with a dollop of buttercream. Then I set that on my cake turntable and spread it with a buttercream the flavor of ginger cookies. When I'd stacked and filled a three-layer cake, I covered it with blue-tinted vanilla buttercream—my base, or crumb coat.

I repeated the process with the eight- and six-inch cake layers. I'd just stuck the smallest cake into my cake fridge when the phone rang again. I could see from the caller ID it was the call I'd been waiting for, and dreading. I picked up. "Hello?"

Friday, October 29, 7 p.m.: Bachelor/bachelorette party! Haunted bonfire and s'mores on Dewey Beach.

I arrived at the bonfire to find Amy opening a bag of marshmallows as Joe hunted for sticks nearby.

"The others are on their way," she said. "Jeez, are you OK?"

"It looks worse than it feels." I had applied all the concealer I owned before leaving my apartment, but it hadn't seemed to make much difference.

"Did you get into a fight with a door?" Joe handed me a stick.

"Heh." I stuffed three marshmallows onto my stick and began toasting.

I stared at the bonfire, almost hypnotized by the flickering flames. And finally, I began to relax.

As kids, the Sea Witch Festival, with its scavenger hunts, parades, and concerts (not to mention its proximity to Halloween) had been a big deal. A children's book of sea myths and legends intensified and confused the interest; for a time, I'd thought ancient civilizations had worshipped the green-faced crone that graced festival balloons.

Amy, Cat, and I loved stories of female sea creatures—mermaids, undines, selkies. Our favorites were the Nereids, the water spirits of Greek mythology. They were beautiful and sometimes fierce, fighting with Poseidon against Dionysus. But they were also kind and helped guide the Argonauts to safety. They lived in a golden palace under the Aegean Sea and were occasionally spotted swimming in the ocean, riding dolphins, or lounging on rocks to dry their sea-green hair, according to Ovid, who wrote, "Nor were their looks the same, nor yet diverse, but like as sisters should be." An illustration in my book had depicted three willowy creatures with long hair—two with dark eyes, like Cat and me, and one with Amy's blue eyes.

What started as a pre-teen obsession became a habit, and for years, we wore long, green wigs, chiffon scarves, and seashell necklaces to the festival. Once, Amy pretended to ride a giant stuffed dolphin. I'd almost called my business Clio Cakes after one of the Nereids, but Cat swore that was the name of an Australian porn star.

I was remembering this when my eyes met those of a man on the far side of the bonfire. My stomach dipped when I recognized Theo Foster. I quickly looked away.

"Sam." Amy nudged me. My marshmallows had dropped into the fire. "Are you OK?"

I smiled at her. "I'm fine," I lied.

Saturday, October 30, 9 a.m.: Breakfast for wedding party and out-of-town guests, followed by costume parade. Sam finishes cake.

I took the rest of the buttercream out of the fridge. I'd applied a thicker layer of blue frosting to the cakes last night after I'd gotten home, and now their smooth, even surfaces were neat and ready for decorating.

I tapped an eight-inch cardboard circle onto the top of the ten-inch cake; I was going to insert several wooden dowels (essential for an upright cake) within the circle. I was trimming a dowel when my doorbell rang. It was Cat, holding a paper bag and two cups of coffee.

"I assume the other guy looks worse," she said.

I'd woken up this morning to find my swollen eye a bright black purple. "It's not going to fade by tomorrow." I couldn't hide the note of panic in my voice.

"I can cover it." Cat sounded confident, but I was doubtful.

"Why aren't you at breakfast with the others?" I waved her in.

"We finished early. I thought you might want some help—" She followed me into the kitchen, and her eyes widened at the jumble of piping bags, tips, and icing knives. I'd also dropped a bowl of buttercream on the floor, leaving frosting and a greasy slick I hadn't yet had time to clean up. "—or company." She handed me a cup of coffee.

Cat perched on a high stool next to my kitchen island, took a sip of coffee, and announced, "You know, Jennifer Ferris was in Ocean City last week." Cat gave a delicate shudder at the thought of Maryland's most famous vacation spot.

That's when I realized what this visit was about. "Oh, yeah?" I tucked a dowel into the cake. "Is that sticking out?"

Cat was not deterred. "Is there something you're not telling me, Sam?"

"Many things."

Cat exhaled loudly, a long-suffering sigh. "Sam. I'm asking you if you went down to the Water View Hotel and Conference Center in Ocean City last week, maybe to interview for a pastry chef position?" She fixed me with her don't-try-to-get-out-of-this-one look.

I sighed. "Yes, I did."

"And?"

"And they just offered me the job. And no, I haven't decided if I'm going to take it yet."

Cat bit into a biscuit. "I thought you said they use vegetable shortening in their frosting and the kitchen is a shambles."

"Yes, I said that."

"And you told us that their chocolate cake uses the worst quality chocolate you've ever tasted. Sam." Cat's expression softened. "What's happened to your business?"

Well, it was failing, that's what happened. "I—"

"This is all Theo Foster's fault," Cat declared, loyally but incorrectly. Theo was a one-time good friend and now an awkward acquaintance. We had met at Marjolaine Bakery on Rehoboth Avenue, where we'd both frosted cupcakes and tried our hands at puff pastry as teenagers. Marjolaine was owned by Theo's aunt, and he'd eventually bought her out. Meanwhile, I'd gone to culinary school, then worked in DC for a few years. When I'd come home and started baking wedding cakes in my kitchen, Theo and I had been friendly. We were the only people in town interested in talking about brown butter.

But then, last year, I'd submitted a proposal (and many cake samples) to The Blue Hen in the hopes of becoming their wedding cake supplier. The Blue Hen is Rehoboth Beach's nicest boutique hotel, and it hosts a lot of weddings—an average of two a weekend from June through October. The contract would have provided me with a steady source of income for nearly half the year.

I'd thrown myself into the pitch, developing a sample menu of mix-and-match cake, filling, frosting, and decoration options, and plying the catering manager with my special Three-Bean (vanilla, coffee, and chocolate) Mousse, not to mention a buttermilk cake with homemade lemon curd filling. My cakes weren't elaborate, but they were elegant and appealing, I thought. And they tasted great.

But in the end, the hotel had given the business to Theo. And now, he supplied them with croquembouches and petit fours. A classic croquembouche, in case you don't know, is a tall, pyramid-shaped, tower of cream puffs, stuck together with caramel. Theo's are dotted with gold dragées, and he tops each with a sugar-work bride and groom, I hear. Very elegant.

I mean, I don't hate him. All's fair in love and pastry. But I'd only found out he had applied for the contract when the hotel called to tell me they'd offered him the job. Theo had called me the following day, but I'd felt betrayed, mostly because I hadn't known we were rivals. Since then, things had been awkward between us. Theo was friendly with Joe and had been invited to the wedding, but I didn't know if he was going.

To top it all off, the past summer—usually peak wedding (and wedding cake) season—had lagged. Two months ago, I'd run through my meager savings and started to run up serious credit card debt. So I'd decided it was time to cut my losses and get a job.

"I can still bake wedding cakes on the side," I said. I dotted buttercream on top of the doweled cake, then carefully stacked the eight-inch one on top.

"It's a part-time job?"

"No," I admitted. "It's full time." Which meant I would not have any time to bake wedding cakes on the side, and we both knew it.

Cat grabbed my hand. "I'm really sorry, Sam. You make wonderful wedding cakes."

I was about to cry, so I turned away and headed to the fridge. That's when I slipped on the spilled buttercream and blackened my other eye.

Sunday, October 31, 8:30 a.m.: Sam takes the cake to Amy's parents' house.

Amy's parents' place—a shingled house on almost half an acre in The Pines—was abuzz when I arrived early Sunday morning. Amy's mom gasped aloud when she saw me. "Samantha! What happened to you?"

"Baking is dangerous work." I kissed her cheek. "I'll just bring the cake into the kitchen."

I was fitting the cake into the rented mini-fridge when Amy's wedding coordinator, a dapper man named Miles, walked in. "Holy smokes, were you in a car accident?"

I handed him a list of printed instructions and told him to find me at once if there were any problems with the cake. Then, trying to hide my battered face from the party rental and catering staff rushing around the house, I escaped upstairs to Amy's old room.

Sunday, 9 a.m.: Bridal party meets at Amy's parents' house.

Amy, in yoga pants and a sports bra, was eating tortilla chips when I opened the door. She stared at me.

"You look relaxed," I said brightly.

"Please tell me you didn't get a second black eye," Amy said.

Sunday, 11:50 a.m.: Music starts—bridal party to top of the stairs.

At last, we were all ready. Amy always looked pretty, but her sea witch's green glass crown seemed to catch the sun and envelop her in refracted light. She looked luminous, a Nereid come to shore.

She stared at us. "You both look beautiful," she sniffled. She crammed the last tortilla chip into her mouth.

Cat and I tottered to the mirror in our silver heels. Our long dresses of blue-gray tulle with ruched bodices and off-the-shoulder sleeves made us look romantically windswept; we were almost as sea nymph-y as Amy with the beach glass hair vines in our hair. And thanks to Cat's cosmetics prowess, my injuries were nearly invisible.

I turned to her. "Thank you, Cat!"

"Don't cry!" Cat looked appalled. "Your makeup's not waterproof!"

12 p.m.: Wedding! Reception immediately to follow.

The ceremony, in the large back garden, was short and beautiful. Amy looked so stunning that everyone simultaneously burst into applause when she appeared, and Joe wiped his eyes.

Afterward, the guests were herded into the living room, where waitstaff circulated with canapes and Champagne. Out in the garden, we posed for photographs while caterers set up tables and a portable dance floor with practiced speed. I discreetly watched as they brought out my cake.

"It looks beautiful," Cat murmured. She was right; the cake was really something. The top tier was the pale, almost shimmery blue of Amy's dress. The middle tier was a deeper baby blue, and the bottom one was a soft blue gray. To finish it off, I'd piped a pattern of white buttercream seahorses, starfish, and shells onto the sides of each tier. "You should be proud, Sam." She squeezed my arm; I squeezed back.

When the photos were finished, Miles led all the guests back into the garden for Amy and Joe's first dance. Joe put the stuffed parrot on his shoulder, and we applauded as they took the floor for "Beyond the Sea."

I took some pictures with my phone and had just grabbed some canapes when someone tapped me on the shoulder. "Hi, Sam." I turned to find Theo Foster smiling at me. "Your cake looks great," he said. "It's good to see you. Do you have a minute?"

I nodded, wishing I hadn't just popped an entire goat cheese tartlet into my mouth.

"Look, I wanted to tell you—" He paused. "I quit the Blue Hen gig. No more croquembouches for me." Theo ran his fingers through his hair. "I gave notice a few days ago, and I told them if they were smart, they'd offer you the contract."

I just stared at him. I was still chewing.

"I told them I thought your wedding cakes were the best in the area and that we'd worked together, and I could vouch for your professionalism."

I finally swallowed. "But we last worked together when we were seventeen," was all I could think of to say. "And I used to call out sick at the last minute whenever Cole Ronovic asked me to tutor him in French."

"I know," Theo said. "I didn't mention that you used to have a crush on that dope. I just wanted to let you know because the catering coordinator is going to call you on Monday."

"Oh, Theo. But why did you—"

"Are you crying?" He looked horrified.

"No! Of course not," I sniffled. "Theo, I'm really grateful. Thank you for recommending me."

"You don't have to be grateful. This job—"

"And now, please join the happy couple on the dance floor!" Miles shouted.

People began to drift toward Amy and Joe, and I heard a loud "Samantha!" It was Jean and Gene, an elderly married pair who lived down the street. They were very friendly, but Jean was hard of hearing, so conversation with them could be strenuous.

Theo was still standing next to me, so I introduced them. Jean winked at him and said to me, "We'll be at your wedding next! Do you have a man friend, Sam?"

"Not at the moment, no."

"You shouldn't ask her that, Jean," Gene said. "She might be a lesbian."

"What?"

"SHE SAID SHE DOESN'T HAVE A MAN FRIEND," Gene boomed. Then he added, "YOU SHOULDN'T ASK HER THAT, YOU KNOW. SHE COULD BE A LESBIAN."

"I'm not a lesbian," I said, but softly. I didn't want anyone nearby to think I was anti-lesbian.

"OR SHE COULD BE ONE OF THOSE ASEXUALS," Gene added. "SOMEONE WHO ISN'T INTERESTED IN SEX. REMEMBER, JEAN? WE READ ABOUT IT ON THE AOL," he explained.

"I'm not asexual," I said, more loudly this time. I could tell I was turning red.

"OR SHE COULD BE A HERMAPHRODITE," Gene hollered. "THAT'S SOMEONE WHO HAS BOTH MALE AND FEMALE SEX ORGANS."

"I'M NOT A HERMAPHRODITE!" I shouted desperately, just as the song ended. In the sudden silence, all eyes turned toward me.

"You don't have to yell, you know," Gene said reproachfully. "She's just a little hard of hearing." Shaking his head, he led Jean away.

I was mortified, but Theo just grinned at me. "So you're single?" The music picked up again—it was Dusty Springfield singing "The Look of Love." "Want to dance?" he asked. Then, I swear, he blushed.

"Sure." I said. "I'd love to."

ELIZABETH MICHAELSON MONAGHAN IS A WRITER AND EDITOR WHOSE WORK HAS APPEARED IN *CITY LIMITS*, *PASTE*, AND *LIBRARY JOURNAL*, AMONG OTHERS. A MENTION OF REHOBOTH BEACH'S SEA WITCH FESTIVAL IN AN ONLINE ENCYCLOPEDIA PROVIDED THE INSPIRATION FOR "THE NEREID'S WEDDING," AND SHE HOPES TO ATTEND THE FESTIVAL SOON. YOU CAN VIEW SOME OF HER NONFICTION AT HTTPS://ELIZABETHMICHAELSON. WORDPRESS.COM. SHE LIVES IN NEW YORK CITY WITH HER HUSBAND, SON, AND MANY TOY TRUCKS.

JUDGE'S COMMENT

Hapless professional baker Samantha encounters a series of unfortunate trials and tribulations, as well as comic half-humiliations, before finally finding the potential for new love in the arms of a fellow baker who has just also—and equally unexpectedly—rescued her business. The humorous touches in this entertaining story are capped by a laugh-out-loud scene toward the end, which balances out the sweetness with comedic texturing.

Life Starts on Tiptoes

By Lonn Braender

Lights flash, buzzers blare, bells clang, and shrieks of delight engulf us. Terence's eyes explode in wonder. The flashing neon lights turn his cheeks into a kaleidoscope of colors. The excitement is infectious. Terence stands oh so tall, stretching higher than ever. He secretly rises on his tiptoes, doing everything in his power to touch that plywood finger—the one that reads "you must be this tall." His hair brushes the sign and he rockets up, nearly dislodging the sign. He's in.

* * * * *

I had a first step and a first word, but I don't remember those. The first milestone I do remember was that one at Funland in Rehoboth Beach.

I'd have done anything to get on that pirate ship ride with all those screaming kids. The big ship swung so high, how it didn't dump them out, I didn't know. The ruckus started at the very first jolt and climaxed at the apex, where the kids stretched their arms high in the air and squealed in glee.

When I finally sat on that cold bench and the metal bar locked against my lap, I thought I'd burst. The huge ship swung low and slow at first, then rolled back and forth, gaining speed with each pass. As it approached the first summit, I let go and lifted my arms high. At the apex, I rose clear off my seat. Terror slammed through me like lightning. That thin, silver bar was the only thing keeping me from plunging to my death. I panicked and clamped down on the bar with all my might. Like everyone else, I screamed, but mine wasn't one of excitement—it was an uncontrollable scream for my life.

*****

One year after that momentous ride, maybe two, my dad let me walk by myself to the boardwalk ice cream stand. I felt so grown up. Sure, I was nervous, but I didn't tell my dad. I laugh now, remembering how I thought I'd hidden my apprehension with a stoic facade.

I had exactly enough money for the ice cream in one pocket and "emergency" money in the other. My mom explained emergency money to me twice. I remember nodding, but I was too excited to listen.

I didn't walk—I ran—to the Double Scoop and had to stand on tiptoes to reach the counter. I agonized about which flavor to pick, deciding on strawberry. I grabbed the cone with one hand and reached for my money with the other. Then, as if in slow motion, that perfect scoop of strawberry listed to one side. I clenched my teeth, eyes wide, and watched as it toppled off the cone, glanced off my toothpick leg, and smashed onto the boardwalk. I forced my tears back, though my lip began to quiver. I willed myself to be the "big boy" my mom had just called me.

A woman who reminded me of my nana scooped up the mess with a napkin and wiped my leg. The lady behind the counter handed me a new cone, telling me to use two hands. I held it tight and thought I might have to give her my emergency money, but my hands were full and she had already turned to the next customer, so I slowly backed away.

The following summer, Mom let me walk the boardwalk with my new friend, Guy. I was determined, albeit with some trepidation, to walk around the world. I'd seen people walk off in one direction and then see them later, coming back from the other. I convinced Guy that the boardwalk circled the world and if we walked this way, we'd see more arcades and ice cream shops than we could count. I might have even hinted that some were free. Imagine my confusion when not five minutes later, the boardwalk abruptly ended. Where were all the other pizza shops, Funlands, and Double Scoops?

With imagined confidence, I convinced Guy to try again, this time walking in the opposite direction. Much to the consternation of a young explorer, ten minutes later, the boardwalk abruptly ended again. How did those people do it? Was there some sort of secret that I didn't know about?

A few years later, I became fascinated by the lifeguards. They were muscled and powerful and important; they swam outside the flags. Lifeguards were lackadaisical, yet they noticed everything. And the girls, holy cow, there were tons of pretty girls, smiling and waving and always talking to the lifeguards. I hung around that white lifeguard chair for an entire summer. Now I knew what I wanted to be when I grew up.

Not all milestones happened in Rehoboth—there was my first home run, first clothes from the men's department, and the eye-opener—the talk from Dad. Holy cow, I couldn't look my mom in the eye for weeks. The next important milestone was becoming a lifeguard. Surprise! Lifeguards aren't superhuman; heck, we were kids working on tans. But at sixteen, in super-cool red shorts, an all-powerful whistle around my neck, and sitting on that sky-high white chair—I was *the man*. Cool enough that I kissed my first girl, right behind the lifeguard chair.

At that age, milestones racked up fast: getting my driver's license, shaving, and, believe it or not, getting fired from a job. That wasn't one I wanted to share.

A special milestone that still makes me smile was my first date. Dad let me take the car so I could take out Rachelle (remember that girl I kissed?). We spent a hot summer day splashing around at Jungle Jim's. Afterward, I gladly splurged two weeks' allowance for chop suey and Cokes. I was a nervous mess. I dropped keys, ran over the curb—I was sure it was my first and *last* date.

And guess what? As klutzy as I'd been, Rachelle thought I was cute. We dated for two summers.

Rachelle couldn't come to Rehoboth the summer before college. We saw each other only once that summer, but we talked on the phone. My mom thought it was for the best—I was headed to Virginia for college and Rachelle was off to Vermont. We tried to keep in touch, but failed miserably. Besides, I wasn't ready for what the next milestone could have been. Soon enough, I was dating other girls. But I never really fell in love with any of them; none of them matched up. Rachelle was the standard I measured every girl against, and I missed her. But I'd been stupid and had stopped calling.

Thinking back, those years were overflowing with tiptoe moments. I'd gotten drunk, smoked pot, and pierced my ear. I made true friends, not just playmates. I'd fallen in and out of love. I can't say that college held more milestones than high school, but I did have many new adventures. I'd grown up and matured, and by graduation, I liked who I'd become. But I often felt like there was something missing, something important.

The summer after graduation, and before starting my first nine-to-five, was my last summer in Rehoboth. I'd worked hard and done well, so sunbathing and bodysurfing were warranted rewards, and reading without a highlighter, heaven.

The saying goes: you'll find what you're looking for when you stop looking. I bumped into, well, ran after, Rachelle that summer. My heart jolted and my breath caught when I saw her sauntering by the water's edge. The way she walked, *eeyoouu*, made my heart skip a beat—again! I didn't understand all my feelings, but I knew I had to catch up to her. When I did, I fumbled and stuttered. She laughed; she was always so confident.

By then, counting milestones had become a game I enjoyed. Most of the time, I realized a milestone soon after it occurred. That first nine-to-five I mentioned was with Google. I took the job as a junior coder because it paid more than lifeguarding. I'd studied computer science in college and was fairly good at writing internet code. I didn't stay a junior coder long; I was quickly promoted and soon making more money than I ever imagined. I had no idea how life-changing it would be.

Milestones, like everything in life, come in degrees. I know this because once, I'd been pulled over for speeding and thought my life was over. A month later, it was off my list. But what had previously been my biggest milestone paled in comparison to what came next. It took every ounce of my courage, but Rachelle said yes!

On a spectacular September afternoon the following year, instead of in a church, we were married on the beach in Rehoboth. It was where I had my first kiss, my first date, and where she said *I do* next to that same lifeguard chair she sauntered past, trying to catch the eye of a gangly, whistle-clad boy.

I told Rachelle that our wedding topped my milestone list and she agreed. As it turned out, we were both so wrong. The birth of Jamal, our perfect son, far outranked anything and everything. I still cannot fully comprehend what happened that day. When I held my son, not twenty minutes old, my heart seemed to double in size. The tears that flowed down my cheeks weren't those of sadness. They originated deep in my heart, flowed through my soul, and spilled out to bathe my son. I became a man, a father.

Some say your first is always your favorite—everything is so new, so exciting, so memorable. They're so wrong. The second time, the day my little princess was born, my heart overflowed with just as much love. Don't get me wrong, Jamal is my world, but having a little girl? Well, there are no words. It was like my heart stood on its own tiptoes, trying to be big enough for two.

We spent every vacation we had in Rehoboth, in a bungalow my folks rented on Maryland Avenue. As my kids grew, I wondered would they solo it to the Double Scoop or explore the end of the boardwalk? Would their lives start on tiptoes at Funland?

As our kids got older, milestones were now coming fast and furious, but they were no longer mine. Promotions, houses, illnesses; my events were no longer significant. My kids were racking up the important milestones, and I watched with sheer delight as they explored the world. To them, everything was a milestone. Had I been like that? Was not getting the lead in the school play really that huge? To my kids, grades, friends, dating, wins and losses, class ranking—everything was important, life changing, even.

My next personal milestone was with my dad. It was cancer and discovered far too late. The day he died was, and remains, the hardest day in my life. Nothing had prepared me. I'd lost loved ones before, so I thought I understood grief. But nothing compared to the loss of my father. As full and expansive as my heart felt when Jamal was born, it felt equally crumpled and deflated as I buried my dad.

After the funeral, a friend told me that we don't actually grow up until we've lost our parents. At the time, I thought it an incredibly insensitive comment. Several years later, when my mom couldn't beat pneumonia, I understood those words. That milestone, losing my mother, felt like a headstone crushing me. I thought losing my dad was hard and that I'd be ready for my mom's passing. I wasn't. But this time, I let myself cry. And as I stood on tiptoes to close the casket, I grew up.

What I hadn't realized until then was that parents are our bedrock;

we build our lives upon them. When I was young, it drove me crazy how they continually meddled in my life. What I hadn't remembered were the innumerable times I sought their wisdom, acceptance, and protection—the countless times I sought their comfort and support. When parents pass, we transform their lives into our own foundation and we realize that we are now the bedrock for our own kids.

As Rachelle and I morphed into our parents, we continued to record milestones, most of which belonged to our kids and most we expected. We did our best to not tell our kids what to do, but rather attempted to steer them through the maze of life to learn for themselves—much like how my dad hadn't walked me to that ice cream shop, even though he knew I'd have to stand on tiptoes to reach the counter. I can picture him today, standing on his own tiptoes to see over the crowd as that precious cone tumbled to the ground.

After the kids went away to college, it didn't take long for Rachelle and I to reclaim our own lives. We fell back in love, and we made love again. Sure, we both had a few extra pounds, but if that was the only casualty of raising two amazing kids, we rejoiced.

One day, helping Rachelle up off the floor where we'd made love, I held her at arm's length and studied her. She blushed, but I was stunned by her beauty. She tried to turn away, but I stopped her. I reminded her what a beautiful and amazing woman she was, and how humble I felt next to her. I wrapped my arms around her and thanked her with tears, and my heart swelled as it had the day she gave me a son.

I had considered all our children's milestones, small or large, important or not, as my own. But they weren't mine. My tiptoe moments had been the years raising two wonderful children, a milestone that spanned twenty-some years. But we weren't ready to let go, so we schemed. We knew the kids would need summer jobs, and even though we each had only three weeks' vacation, we rented a place for the summer in Rehoboth. They could get jobs in a shop or a restaurant, or maybe even be a lifeguard.

We found a small house not far from the one my parents rented for all those summers, and it felt like going home. That summer, we watched our kids mature; they worked long hours and saved their money. They exercised and ate organic; they discussed current events and debated issues; they learned how to play bridge. I was so proud to see them transform into adults. Rachelle laughed at me. Unlike me, she'd always known the kids would prosper.

We rented that same house each year until they finished college. Odd how life works sometimes. Right after college tuition ended, that house on Maryland Avenue became available. We bought that bungalow, even though it was overpriced.

Soon after that, milestones began piling up again. Jamal married an incredible young woman; she was Rachelle reincarnated. But the following year, my daughter got engaged to a punk, and I was pissed. The guy was rough and moronic; he called me by my given name. And his hair was longer than my daughter's.

Before the wedding, Rachelle handed me an old photograph of a scruffy young man, hair to his shoulders, sitting on the beach surrounded by a gang of hoodlums. She told me to take a good look because that bedraggled guy there was me. The photo is on my dresser to this day. It turned out the boy wasn't such a punk after all, and truth be told, I'm a little jealous of his hair.

With the kids on their own, I thought our milestones would slow. No way—apartments, jobs, weddings, and fights were all tiptoe moments. And like us, our kids didn't wait to have kids of their own. When Terence was born, my son became a man, just as I had. I saw his heart expand, and I saw him shed a tear, something he hadn't done since he was thirteen. I understood what had just happened; it was a life-changing moment.

Terence, my namesake, was the first. A year later, my daughter had sweet little Rachelle. So now, both my kids understood the milestone of bringing a life into this world—now they got it. It was amazing to see them transform into parents. Had my folks noticed that change in me? I laugh at myself; of course they had.

With the expanding family, we had to rethink the beach house. I started to complain, as my dad had once done. I griped and wondered aloud where everyone would sleep. Rachelle just stared at me, one eyebrow raised, hand on hip. It didn't matter where, as long as it was here, with us. And it didn't take much to talk the kids into coming to Rehoboth. Soon enough, it became what we loved. Every chance we found, we squeezed the grandchildren and their parents into the bungalow.

*****

Lights flash, buzzers blare, bells clang, and shrieks of delight engulf us. Terence's eyes explode in wonder. The flashing neon lights turn his cheeks into a kaleidoscope of colors.

Terence rises on tiptoes, making the briefest of contact with the plywood finger. He leaps in delight. My heart swells, and I laugh and chase after him to the pirate ship ride. I ask Terence where he wants to sit, and of course, he points to that same last row I had chosen, the one that reaches high in the sky. I hope he lifts his arms high and squeals with glee. That's a hope—and a prayer—that won't end when the pirate ship gradually slows and comes to a stop.

LONN BRAENDER IS A JERSEY-BORN ARTIST, PRINTER, BUSINESSMAN, ENTREPRENEUR, AND NOW, WRITER. A PAINTER OF LANDSCAPES AND SEASCAPES FOR MORE THAN TWENTY-FIVE YEARS, HE RECENTLY FACED CHANGES THAT FORCED HIM TO FIND AN ALTERNATIVE CREATIVE OUTLET. WRITING HAS FILLED THAT NEED AND HAS BECOME HIS PASSION. LONN HAS WRITTEN A DOZEN OR MORE WORKS OF VARYING LENGTH, AND HAD HIS FIRST PUBLISHED WORK IN THE 2016 ANTHOLOGY, *BEACH NIGHTS*. "LIFE STARTS ON TIPTOES" IS HIS SECOND PUBLISHED WORK. LONN LIVES IN WASHINGTON CROSSING, PENNSYLVANIA WITH HIS LIFELONG MUSE AND CRITIC, BOTH OF WHOM PLAN TO SOMEDAY CALL REHOBOTH BEACH HOME.

Secrets

By Amber Tamosaitis

"This place isn't bad," Scott said, paddling past me on his bodyboard. "Yeah, I like it," I replied. "It's really nostalgic for me."

I smiled as I gazed back toward the beach. Bursts of blue umbrellas and vibrantly colored beach blankets splashed against the shimmering sand. Beach houses and shops painted in shades of sand, sky, and grass formed a pastel backdrop. Rehoboth had changed since I was little, and yet, so much was the same. The warm water, rising and falling gently around me, began to lull me into a wistful reverie.

One that didn't last.

"Eek!"

The shriek that escaped my lips shocked me. But it was mine. Something had tugged at the back of my bikini top, then quickly let go. It wasn't painful, but the strap made a small smack and caught me off guard. I whirled around just as Scott's bodyboard tapped my side. He had that stupid, innocent grin on his face. I tried to push the bodyboard away, but he was too quick. I settled on splashing water at him as meager payback.

"You scared me, you jerk!"

"You just looked so cute, the way you were standing there, deep in thought."

"I'm glad you find that cute." I took another shot at him. I could feel the water pull a little out to sea and my feet begin to sink farther into the mud.

"I'll be back, babe. Looks like a good one." With that, Scott paddled toward the burgeoning wave.

I began paddling sideways, as the wave seemed to be coming in at an angle. Enjoying a calm spot in the ocean, I managed to avoid the breaking of the wave and let my lower half sink in, the water enveloping my body up to my chest. I sighed contentedly and closed my eyes.

"Nice out here, isn't it?" a voice nearby remarked.

"Yeah," I said with a contented sigh, not bothering to open my eyes.

"Good day to hit the beach."

"Yup."

"And you've brought a good-lookin' one with you this time."

I opened my eyes and looked around.

"What?"

I could feel the waves rippling around me, but as I turned, I couldn't find the owner of the voice.

"Though this one's no comparison to that one you brought ten years ago. What was his name? Dennis? Dave?"

"What?"

I could feel my shoulders tense up. Did she mean Dylan? I met him when I was in high school. We were down here for the summer and—

"Are you going to try and go skinny-dipping with this one, too?"

Definitely Dylan.

"Who are you? How did you know Dylan and I did that?" I demanded.

The voice chuckled, and I began to look around, frantically.

"Oh, *Dylan*. That was his name. I'll have to remember that."

"Where are you?"

"I'm right here. Oh, look, here comes the new guy. I should tell him about Dylan. Or maybe about some of your other little summer flings."

I spun around and shot my hand into the water in the direction of the voice, but found nothing.

"Stop screwing around!"

"Babe?" Scott called from behind me. "What's wrong?"

"Nothing," I replied tentatively. "Nothing. I'm just ready to get out."
I started to trudge past him, then turned back and took his hand.
"Come with me?"

He eyed me, then followed, his bodyboard in tow. As we were nearing the point where the waves broke, he let go of my hand. I turned back to see his bodyboard disappear below the water's surface. As he yanked on the cord, it broke and the bodyboard flipped, then began floating away from us, against the water's current and at a swift pace, as if being pulled.

I grabbed his wrist and guided him back to the shore, my legs pumping as hard as they could.

* * * * *

"I thought you *wanted* to come to the beach."

"I did—I mean, I do. I want to be here."

Scott scooted closer to the table. "Then why are you acting all freaked out? Is it because of the voice in the ocean?"

I tensed up. After we'd gotten out of the water, I'd tried to explain what had happened—well, certain parts of it—but he laughed at me, said I was being paranoid. Of course I was. But I still couldn't shake the feeling that I was being watched. And that made it hard to relax.

Our outdoor table overlooked the bay. People were coming in on boats and stepping up to the dock to be greeted by a host. My family had never had the money for such a luxury, but sitting here and enjoying the scene, I felt like royalty. Slowly, I began to relax and forget the weird occurrence at the beach.

"You still up for goin' out on the boat with Marty tomorrow?" Scott asked, a couple of glasses of wine and a meal later.

"Yeah, of course."

"Just checking. You know, after today, I don't want you freaking out when the boat's already out on the water."

"I won't," I said with more certainty than I felt.

"I mean, I had been hoping we could get in some quality time on the water tonight," he said, producing a set of unfamiliar keys from his pocket.

"I cannot believe Marty let you have those."

"Spare pair. He owes me."

I looked down. I could feel Scott's eyes on me, expectantly. But considering that I already felt uneasy about going out on the water in broad daylight tomorrow, I was sure there was no way I could enjoy myself out on the boat with Scott in the dark of night. I would rather keep our romantic getaway on land as much as possible.

Scott must have understood. He slid the keys back into his pocket and leaned back in his chair.

"Still, 'voices in the ocean' sounds like a ghost story or something."

"Yeah, maybe for someone like Nancy Drew." I took a drink.

He patted my hand and rose from his seat. "Gonna run to the bathroom."

I sighed as he walked away. I couldn't help but feel he was patronizing me with that last gesture. Gullible little Erin, always so easily scared or fooled.

I scooted my chair toward the edge of the dock and gazed over the railing. Boats passed leisurely over the glistening water as music came through a speaker on the restaurant's roof. As the sun dropped to kiss the horizon, the sky and the water that reflected it had leisurely shifted from azure to a golden orange.

"So what'd he say about Dylan? I mean, you two are having such a nice dinner, I guess he took it well."

I jumped back, almost toppling out of my chair.

"Assuming you told him, that is."

"Wh-what do you want?" I whispered, looking around.

"Look, I've got plenty of ammunition here. Dylan might have been your first, but that next summer, there was Tony, then Mike, then Jack—"

"You mean Tommy, Mick, and Josh—er, I mean, how do you know all this?"

Oh God, people are staring at me talking to . . . talking to . . . whom?

I settled in my chair and pulled it closer to the table. I poured what was left of our bottle of wine into my glass and took a big gulp. Slowly, the curious faces began to turn away.

"Wine? Wasn't it that Bobby guy who got you drinking that stuff? A real class act, that one. Local craft beer and a taste for fine wine."

I could feel my toes curl in my sandals.

"The toe-curl. I've seen that, too."

I looked down at the floor beneath my feet. Between the planks of wood, I could see water. Just water. No malevolent face staring back at me, waiting to unleash all my summer secrets.

"I don't know who you are—or where you are—but please leave me alone."

"I can't do that. Not yet, at least."

"Then when?"

"When you do something for me, I'll be glad to leave you to your little weekend getaway."

I lowered my head so it was slightly below the table. "What is it you want?"

"Babe?"

Scott's voice made me jump, causing me to bang my head on the edge of the table.

"What are you doing?"

"Um . . ."

"You feeling okay?"

"No, actually. I think, I guess I just had a little too much wine."

"You gonna be sick?"

"No, I'm just . . . just gonna head back to the hotel."

I rose from the table and began making my way toward the exit. As I did, I heard the voice softly say, "Meet me where your friend Marty's boat is docked. Come after the sun is gone and the moon is high. I'll be waiting."

* * * * *

I don't know if it was some combination of bodyboarding and wine or what, but Scott fell asleep not long after we got into bed. Meanwhile, I lay awake, trying to process the bizarre series of events. Somehow, my romantic weekend getaway had been hijacked by a mysterious blackmail scheme. Who was this person? Why couldn't I see her? And what did she want?

It was enough to make a girl paranoid.

I delicately slid out of bed, although it probably didn't matter. Scott's snoring was loud, but rhythmic. He was out for the night.

I threw on my clothes from the previous day, grabbed my purse and Scott's spare keys to Marty's boat, and a little after midnight, slipped out of the hotel room.

There were still a fair number of people out and about. The dock, however, was quiet.

Marty's boat was small but comfortable. He had plenty of seating above and a small area below for his passengers to relax. I had gone out plenty of times with Scott and Marty. However, I now stood there in anticipation of what lay in my immediate future.

"I'm here," I said in a low voice.

"I appreciate your punctuality."

"What do you want me to do?"

"Get in the boat."

"I should untie it first."

"No need for that. This won't take long."

A shiver ran down my spine. I looked at the boat, and suddenly it seemed all too small. Too accessible from all sides by the water. The damned water, the one source I could tie to this voice.

"Oh no, you aren't afraid, are you?"

The voice chuckled again, a snide, high-pitched laugh, one that was absolutely at my expense.

"Why should I trust you?"

"Look, you humans spend every summer depositing your waste in my home. The least you can do is this one task for me."

I looked around, then tentatively stepped into the boat.

"OK . . ."

"Go down into the lower room and tell me what you see there."

Hesitantly, I placed the smaller key into the lock on the door. I held my breath, not sure what I was going to see inside. The ship creaked and swayed beneath my feet, and my stomach began to turn. I took a deep breath and thrust open the door.

I peered into the musty darkness, fumbled for the light switch, and flicked it on.

No dead body. Just the same wood paneling the boat had had since Marty bought it, a futon with sheets that looked like they hadn't been washed in equally as long, and a mini-fridge just below a liquor cabinet. I returned to the deck.

"Um, it looks normal. Messy, but normal."

"Good," the voice said. "Check the liquor cabinet, and see if he still has some of that rum left in there."

"What?"

The boat began to sway violently.

"Just do it."

I hurried back below and, sure enough, there was a half-finished bottle of rum. I grabbed it and rushed back up to the surface.

"He's got some. Here it is."

"Great. Toss it into the water, starboard side."

"But—"

"Hurry up. Toss the bottle in. And make sure the cap is on good and tight."

I walked to the edge of the boat opposite the dock and hesitated.

"What's wrong?"

I wasn't sure, but I thought I saw ripples in the water. Ripples and . . . Something broke the surface for a moment. I strained my eyes, but it disappeared below the surface before I got a good look. I could hear the water splashing, but even in the light of the moon couldn't make anything out.

"You won't need that rum anyway," the voice assured me. "This boat isn't going anywhere for a while."

"What do you mean?"

"I got under there and snapped off the propeller. Don't know a lot about boats, but a broken propeller should keep things quiet for a few days."

"You what? Why?"

"I did it to all the boats, so don't look so mad. You guys can go boating another time. There are more important things to worry about tomorrow."

"Like what?'

The voice sighed. "Just toss it in already and I'll tell you."

I drew in my breath and chucked the bottle into the ocean.

The bottle bobbed about in the water for a few seconds before a head popped up behind it.

"My sister thanks you for this. It'll make a satisfactory drink for her wedding reception tomorrow."

"Wedding . . . reception?"

"Yes, and with the boats silenced, we should be able to enjoy the celebration to our hearts' content."

"You . . . what the—"

"No hard feelings?" The light of the moon caught the edge of her face, which she tilted innocently. Long, wet locks of hair fell past her chin. "It's nothing personal after all."

"Nothing personal? What about all that personal stuff about *me?*"

"You're not the first. We pick up a lot of dirt on people while they're here for vacation. I'm just doing what I can to make use of it."

I had no response. Her head disappeared beneath the water's surface, and then something else flashed above the water. Something that shimmered in the light of the moon and splashed as it came back down. Something that, as it swam away, I was certain looked just like a large fish's tail.

* * * * *

It took me a while to try to make sense of what had happened. A human torso, a fish's tail. And aquatic blackmail for a bottle of rum. A bottle of rum for a mermaid wedding? I fell asleep that night on the boat, trying to parse the mystery of just how mermaids could drink rum beneath the water. I awoke the next morning to find Scott and Marty staring at me with looks of complete confusion. What was I supposed to say to them? How could I ever explain what had happened? In the end, I decided this, too, should be another secret shared only with the sea.

AMBER TAMOSAITIS HAS LOVED WORDS, PARTICULARLY WRITTEN ONES, SINCE EARLY CHILDHOOD. HER LOVE OF READING, WRITING, AND LANGUAGES HAS LED HER TO A CAREER IN JAPANESE-TO-ENGLISH TRANSLATION. MOST OF HER WORK HAS BEEN TRANSLATING MANGA, OR GRAPHIC NOVELS, INTO ENGLISH. "SECRETS" IS HER FIRST SHORT FICTION PUBLICATION, AND SHE IS EXCITED TO BE A PART OF *BEACH LIFE*. FOR MORE INFORMATION, PLEASE VISIT HER WEBSITE AT WWW.AMBTAM.COM.

The Boy on the Bike

By Susan Miller

"Some guy on a bike just tried to bum a cigarette from me."

Janine didn't smoke, but for some reason, she seemed to find the solicitation enthralling, yet funny. Janine, with a perm that bounced in dizzy streaks around her face, puckered up her ruby lips, pulled an imaginary Marlboro from her acid-wash shorts, and puffed make-believe smoke rings at the stars. "A cigarette, from me! No matter," she said. "Ladies, it's time to go in." It was the summer of 1989, and for what could have been the 100th time, we tumbled off the Jolly Trolley on Rehoboth Avenue and giggled our way into Summer House.

We were the denizens of Dewey who could never quite make a night of it standing in ankle-deep beer at the Cork or struggling for a square inch on the Starboard's outdoor deck. We would patronize the Dewey parties at houses with names like Circus, Kahuna, and Beached Whale (at least that was the name Janine gave it when she found her ex-boyfriend's ex-girlfriend passed out on the living room floor). But at some point every Friday night, usually when the mosquitoes started to peck and the air grew thick under a sweaty sky, we'd pile onto the trolley, grill the driver with silly questions ("Has anyone ever fallen out of this thing?"), and head for our mecca—Summer House, the best bar and dance spot in Rehoboth.

We were twenty-three, there were two hours until closing time, and we had never felt this cool.

Janine would lead the way, carefully staking out barstools near the best-looking boys, never tucked in a corner or near the kitchen, and never at a table. "No one is going to ask you to dance if you are sitting at a table" was her mantra. We'd order the House's Long Island Iced Tea, and the four of us would sit there in our Debbie Gibson-like pedal pushers, sipping and pondering the potential for a dance or a midnight stroll on the sand. We'd map our futures on beverage napkins and yap about the first thing we'd look for in a guy: his eyes, his smile, his hair, and for Janine, his shoes. His *shoes?* "Yes," she would say, all business. "A guy can be cool from the ankles up, but the ones who are truly cool care about what kind of shoes they are wearing."

On the rare occasion when one of us did get asked to dance, the others would sit and assess, twirling our rope bracelets and thumping our bleached white Keds against the bar. But most of the time when we'd hear the first strains of "Love Shack," "Like a Prayer," or our anthem, "I Will Survive," Janine would leap off her stool with all of us in tow. Flailing our arms, blaring out the words with wild abandon, we knew there was no place we would rather be at 12:30 a.m. than with our little girl posse at the center of the universe—the dance floor.

"Excuse me, gorgeous, I think you dropped an earring," a voice boomed from behind, cutting into that gloomy moment when the lights flickered on and "Hit the Road Jack" echoed from the DJ booth.

Janine spun around, suddenly face-to-face with the shaggy-haired boy—the cigarette-bumming biker—as he held out a shiny gold hoop like an offering of nectar. Green-blue eyes, a scorpion tattoo crawling over his left shoulder, Birkenstocks. In a nanosecond, I knew our girl was smitten.

"Girls, give me a minute, please," she pleaded, stuffing cash for the tab into our pockets. But then a minute turned into twenty, then thirty as the two teased and toyed, oblivious to the barmaids mopping the tile and the inebriated preppies stumbling toward the door. I watched in awe as the magic stirred between them, a secret lingo that locked them into their own abbreviated universe.

The passions, the possibilities. *This,* I thought, *is what beach nights are all about.*

★ ★ ★ ★ ★

"Do you want sweetener?" The frosty glass that slid across the table—a real iced tea—cut into my reverie.

"Sweetener is fine," I told the waitress. "Hey, do people still dance here?"

The weary server stabbed a finger with a peeling peach nail at me. "Honey, I'm usually out of here by seven. I see a lot of cheeseburgers, bawling babies, and a few locals glued to the Golf Channel," she said. "Who knows what happens in the wee hours."

Well, she was right. Twenty-eight years ago, if someone had told me I'd be sitting in a booth at Summer House drinking plain iced tea and poking at a Caesar salad at 5 p.m., I wouldn't have believed it. This was almost blue plate special time.

Funny how when we had our beach house at Dewey, we never came to Rehoboth to trek the boardwalk, indulge in fudge, or munch Thrasher's fries. We had one pit stop, always at night and always for dancing. Funny how right now, I couldn't even imagine where a DJ would set up.

I sipped my tea and thought of the simple brass urn back at Wall's Cottages where I was staying, just waiting for me as the clock ticked. Somehow, tomorrow, I had to find a way to do this.

I hadn't set foot on the Delaware beaches since that summer of '89. None of us had, really. As we navigated the 90s, our little band dissolved, the way those twenty-something bonds sometimes do. For me, there was nursing school, rotations, a marriage, two kids, and one exhausting divorce.

But one person stood true throughout—Janine. My free-spirited friend who was just as comfortable getting a butterfly tattoo at age thirty as she was wiping my brow when I had a vicious bout of morning sickness. "You held my hand, now I hold yours," she would say. While I was helping my kids negotiate the terrible twos, she was backpacking the Dalmation Coast. Our lives couldn't have grown more different, but our souls were always stitched together. I felt sad for her sometimes, a restless force who could never quite nail things, teetering from job to job, man to man. But in the next breath, I felt inspired. She was always stretching, always seeking the next spark. There were no regrets in Janine's world, and secretly, I wanted to sip from that cup.

No matter what corner of the planet she was on, she would try to make it back for birthdays, christenings, divorce hearings. And if she couldn't, there were emails and instant messages.

And then there were the phone calls, two to be exact. The first from Janine, her voice a bit too husky. Why didn't I get it, realize something was off? Why didn't she just tell me? My endless string of whys. The second from her distant cousin somewhere in Colorado. A call that replayed in my head like a torturous loop in the past nine months. The Colorado cousin ticked off the to-do list: meager bank accounts were shut; the Queens walk-up was cleared out; there would be no funeral, but oh, would there be a way for you to take the ashes?

They came in a cheap brass urn that felt completely un-Janine-like. In a blur, I moved them from room to room, put them in a closet, and then in a basement drawer. "My friend, you are not at all comfortable here," I told her and could just feel her eyes roll.

Over the winter, it hit me. The ocean, the beach. It seemed right, it soothed me. But when I got to Rehoboth twenty-four hours earlier, I was paralyzed.

"You ready for the check, dear?"

The once-gruff server somehow seemed to soften, or maybe I just desperately needed someone's smile. I looked at the wrinkled men at the bar, debating Tiger Woods over bottles of Bud, and the toddler in the high chair happily chomping Cheerios. "Yes, it's time to go," I said. I walked outside into the soupy air and heard a familiar clank as the Jolly Trolley lumbered down Rehoboth Avenue. And then, amazingly, trailing behind the trolley was a guy with graying temples and torn T-shirt, a cigarette clasped between his lips. A guy on a bike. He whooshed by me, then stopped and turned his head. "Ma'am, excuse me, you got a light?"

Oh my God, Janine, I thought, *you have got to be kidding me.* Tomorrow, I promise. I'll do it tomorrow.

SUSAN MILLER IS AN EDITOR/WRITER FOR *USA TODAY* NEWSPAPER. SHE MAJORED IN ENGLISH AT THE UNIVERSITY OF VIRGINIA. POETRY HAS BEEN A HOBBY OF HERS FOR MANY YEARS, AND HER POEMS HAVE APPEARED IN PUBLICATIONS SUCH AS *GEMINI MAGAZINE* AND *COMMON GROUND REVIEW*. SHE DECIDED TO TAKE A BREAK FROM POETRY AND TRY HER HAND AT A SHORT STORY WHEN SHE LEARNED ABOUT THE REHOBOTH BEACH READS CONTEST—SET IN REHOBOTH, ONE OF HER TREASURED VACATION SPOTS.

The Stranger and the Horseshoe

By Alex Hannah

I shiver as I trudge along the sand path, and the orange glow of the sun appears. Having ignored the heavy, loud winds that woke me, I realize I am underdressed and curse to myself that I don't have gloves.

I emerge from the trees of Chesapeake Street and onto Rehoboth Beach. The edges of the ocean turn from darkness to orange as the sun begins its ascent.

The wind blows across the beach; the sand rises and creates a low, yellow fog. I shove my hands into my pockets and speed up, questioning my judgment again.

And then I notice a horseshoe crab lying on its back, lifeless, its brown legs protruding from its giant shell as the sand blows up and over him. In the emerging light, I see more horseshoes down the beach in front of me. I turn on my phone's flashlight; there are dead horseshoes lying on their backs as far as I can see. The previous night's fast-moving storm and a receding tide appear to have caught these animals on their backs, and their many scuttling legs now have grown still.

There must be hundreds of horseshoes on the long beach. I breathe deeply as I stare at the heavily armored creatures, alien-looking shellfish with ancestors that date back hundreds of millions of years.

I say a silent prayer for the fossils that have washed up on the beach and continue my walk.

As night becomes day and the sun unveils the devastation of the horseshoes, I see a hooded figure ahead of me. The person is running away from the beach, and then he bends and grabs a horseshoe, runs back to the ocean, and gently tosses the creature back into the water.

As I approach and yell hello loudly enough to be heard over the crashing waves, the person looks up and stops. He is lightly dressed in jeans and a sweatshirt; his hair is long and unkempt. Both earlobes are pierced with large black plugs, and I see snake tattoos creeping up his neck to his face. I freeze, caught off guard by this stranger on the beach.

He approaches me, smiles, and says, "I'm throwing these things back into the ocean so they can live."

I stare back. "You're wasting your time," I say. "They're all dead."

Undeterred, he points to one and says, "They're alive, and I'm throwing as many back as I can."

I process that for a moment and shrug. "Okay," I say. "Stay warm. And that's a nice thing for you to do."

I continue my stroll down the beach. As the space between the stranger and me increases, I see more and more horseshoes on the beach. Now curious, I approach one and give it a little nudge with my foot. The ancient creature stirs and sluggishly sticks a leg out of its shell. It *is* alive.

I take a deep breath and pick up the awkward horseshoe. Sand blows against my legs as I shuffle slowly toward the shore. The waves hit my feet as I put the crab back in the ocean. The horseshoe turns in the white water, the hard shell rising before it disappears below the surface.

I go back up to the beach, my hands now tingling in the cold, take the next horseshoe, and throw it back into the ocean. I repeat this again and again until I lose track of how many crabs I've returned to the churning water. They slowly struggle as I carefully walk them down to the water and toss them in.

The combination of the chillingly hard shell and the wind make me lose feeling in my fingers. I keep telling myself just one more horseshoe crab, but then I notice another one only a few feet away that needs my help.

As I'm about to rescue another horseshoe, the stranger walks by, headed to Rehoboth. He glances at me and says, "I can't do any more. I think I threw in about fifty."

I nod, thinking that I can do more. The sun has risen, and as we check behind us, we notice that the stretch of beach that had previously been covered with horseshoes is now clear. We squint down the beach toward Rehoboth and see hundreds more horseshoe crabs on their backs and in need of help.

Then we observe other people on the beach, dark forms walking from the beach to the ocean with horseshoes in their hands, tossing them into the water.

I gaze at the stranger and say, "I'm not sure if they got the idea from you, but it looks like others are helping the horseshoe crabs. That's good. Thank you for telling me they could be saved."

He smiles and laughs before he replies, "Is that what they are? I thought they might be horseshoes, but I had never seen one before. When I get home, I'm going to look them up so I can learn more." He then gives me a quick wave and heads toward Rehoboth.

I watch him go. It's quite a thing, I think, to reach out your hand to help a creature when you don't know anything about it—not even its proper name. Then I glance down, pick up the next horseshoe, and hike to the ocean to throw it in.

ALEX HANNAH DREAMS OF REHOBOTH BEACH BUT RESIDES IN WASHINGTON, DC, WITH HIS AMAZING WIFE AND BEST FRIEND, STACY, AND THEIR WHIRLWIND OF A CAT, ROCKET. THIS IS ALEX'S FIRST PUBLISHED WORK, AND HE'S THRILLED THAT IT WAS SELECTED AS HE LOVES TO WRITE. THIS NOT ONLY REINFORCES THE NEED TO SPEND MORE TIME AT THE BEACH, BUT IT ALSO PROVIDES THE PERFECT GIFT FOR EVERYONE HE KNOWS—*EVERYONE*.

JUDGES' COMMENTS

This is a tale of community, of the sea, of the town. The use of first person engages the reader, and while we know the story, the twist is in the character development. A timeless story, well written. In less than a thousand words, this story moves quickly—from the kind of resignation most of us have felt when faced with a similarly sad scene in nature, to a steadfast determination to alter what at first glance appeared inalterable. Hooray for horseshoe crabs, and hooray for this unnamed main character! If dolphins sometimes rescue drowning people, well, people sometimes have an opportunity to return the favor. A gratifying, feel-good read. For those interested in the state of our environment, this story speaks to that issue. It is a sweet story that carries a strong message.

The Bench

By Jenny Scott

It was a favorite ritual.

Every summer evening, he walked the few blocks to his favorite bench, the one at the far, southern end of the boardwalk. It was just past Funland and most of the crowd, and he could hear the gulls overhead and the waves spilling onto the sand, yet still make out the faint ringing of bells of the carnival games, the delighted squeals of children, and excited voices of the adults. He wasn't much for crowds of people these days and had never ridden the pirate ship or played Skee-Ball, but he liked the noise of it all.

Sometimes, his bench was taken.

Sometimes, it was occupied by love-struck high school kids in the middle of a summer romance, looking for somewhere a bit off the beaten path. Sweaty palms. Nervous chatter. Touching elbows ever so slightly and stealing glances at one another underneath the glow of the lamps and moonlight. And that was OK. He remembered being that age. He remembered his own awkward dates and fumbling over words and spilling a piping-hot bucket of Thrasher's fries all over a girl's yellow sundress.

Sometimes, it was occupied by a tired-looking young couple and their screaming kids. Beach totes full of toys. Diaper bags covered in sand. Sunburnt shoulders and hungry stomachs and plastic buckets filled with a prized collection of seashells.

"When are we eating?"

"What's for dinner?"

"Mom, he's taking shells out of my bucket and putting them into his!"

Then the dad would get a pizza, and before long, everyone would be chattering happily about *the best day ever!*

He didn't mind that his bench was taken on those evenings, either. He remembered those long beach days with his own children. Hours spent under a hot sun, wrangling flyaway umbrellas, breaking up squabbles, and making hourly trips to the bathrooms.

Sometimes, the bench was occupied by a young woman, knees curled up beneath her and head bent over a paperback novel. Sometimes, it was occupied by a young man, legs outstretched and arms crossed, deep in thought as he watched the lights of passing ships far out on the horizon. And that was OK. The bench was big enough for two, so he would smile and nod and then sit at the other end. And they usually smiled and nodded back. Sometimes they struck up a conversation—the young woman might tell him what she was reading, or the young man might let him know what he was thinking, and eventually they left as friends.

Sometimes, it was occupied by a couple with matching gray streaks in their hair and lightweight cardigans to protect against the mild summer breeze. They sat close, shoulder-to-shoulder, his hand resting gently on her knee, and they spoke with the soft murmurs of two people who have spent a lifetime sharing their souls with each another. And it was OK that they were on his bench. He remembered sitting there shoulder-to-shoulder with his own gray-haired beauty. Sometimes talking. Sometimes resting in comfortable silence. Usually sharing a bucket of fries. He only spilled them on her that one time, but she still liked to tease him about it.

But tonight. Tonight, the bench was vacant. The crowds were thinning out as summer was drawing to an end. Small groups were still clinging to the last remaining days of the season, trying to squeeze every ounce of memory from the warm, salty air. Real life was just around the corner. They weren't ready to say goodbye.

One last stroll down the boardwalk.

One more chocolate-and-vanilla swirl from Kohr's.

One more time hunting for sand crabs or playing miniature golf or scrounging through one's pockets for quarters to use at the arcade and maybe win enough tickets to take home a big prize.

It's not over yet, they all assured themselves.

For him, it was.

He settled onto the bench, a cane resting across his knees, and the memories of countless summer days came over him like a wave. Just a gentle one—a soft, rolling break of water that lightly washes ashore, revealing bits of shell and stone exposed in the wet sand it leaves behind.

He thought of all the time spent on this bench with his wife, still feeling her warm hand in his. He thought about all the happy days spent here with his family. His grandkids. The echoes of their laughter filled his ears. He felt the taste of vinegar from the fries on his tongue and smelled the breeze coming off the shore. He thought about the strangers he had met and the friends he had made. How his own recollections intersected with the memories of countless others. This bench, this beach, had brought them all together.

But the time had come. The moon glowed brightly overhead, its beams dancing across the rippling waters. The noises in the background had faded away. It was just him out here. Just him and a reminder of a thousand beautiful days. He slowly stood up, cane in hand, and gave the bench one last look.

"Thank you."

And he began his final walk home.

JENNY SCOTT IS A DOG-MOM AND DELAWARE NATIVE WHO LOVES TO TRAVEL BUT ALWAYS LOOKS FORWARD TO RETURNING TO HER HOME STATE. SHE GRADUATED FROM THE UNIVERSITY OF DELAWARE WITH A DEGREE IN HISTORY AND IS PRESENTLY EMPLOYED DOING MARKETING AND RECRUITING FOR A HOME CARE COMPANY. ON THE SIDE, SHE ENJOYS BLOGGING AND IS CURRENTLY WORKING ON AN ILLUSTRATED CHILDREN'S BOOK. THE INSPIRATION FOR HER STORY CAME FROM HER OWN CHILDHOOD DAYS AT THE BEACH, HOW TRADITIONS CONTINUE FROM GENERATION TO GENERATION, AND THE MEMORIES MADE ARE SHARED BY FRIENDS AND STRANGERS ALIKE.

JUDGE'S COMMENT

Sense of place and atmosphere, and an elegiac sense of time. The growing sense that something is, perhaps, amiss, that time may be about to play a more significant role in this tale, that mortality may take a bow. And then that final, ambiguous line. As in life itself, we are left to wonder....

We Found Buried Pirate Treasure!

By Douglas Harrell

Pirate ships were once a dreaded and all-too-common sight off Cape Henlopen. What you and thousands of other visitors to the fabulous and storied beaches of Rehoboth and Lewes don't know, dear reader, is that they still are. The story of the intrepid treasure hunters who made this remarkable discovery, and who tracked down treasure chests loaded with booty, spans more than two decades and can only now be told.

Our story begins innocently enough on Lewes Beach in 1996. After a fun day in the water and a nice dinner, our unsuspecting little band crossed the dunes and returned to the water's edge for a relaxing, postprandial stroll. I was leading the way, followed by my wife, Carolyn, Grandpa George, Grandma Jo, and sisters-in-law, Ann and Beth, with their husbands, John and Bill. Bringing up the rear were my niece Amy, age seven, and my nephew Billy, age four (Beth's kids), and my nephew Jonathan (John's son), age sixteen and Amy and Billy's hero.

Before we had advanced ten yards, I spied something bobbing in the water. It appeared to be an old bottle that had been sealed with a cork.

"I see something in the water," I cried. Not loudly enough, apparently, as Amy and Billy were still occupied, looking for shells and throwing little clumps of dried seaweed at each other.

Thankfully, Grandma Jo came to the rescue at close to 90 decibels.

"Billy, look!" she exclaimed, while crouching slightly and pointing.

That did the trick. Now both Amy and Billy were eagerly waiting at the water's edge as I lunged into the crashing surf to recover the object that had so aroused our curiosity (in point of fact, that's a bit of an exaggeration, but it provides a better mental image for you, dear reader, than me wading up to my knees and plucking it off of a preternaturally calm Delaware Bay.)

It was indeed an old bottle, and Billy, looking closely, said, "There's a message inside!"

After some effort and the assist of a small, scavenged stick, I was finally able to extract a stiff and delicate piece of paper (all the while making a mental note to remember to bring tweezers with me on any future walks during which it seemed likely we might find a bottle with a message in it).

I carefully unrolled the paper. It was brown and brittle, and burned around the edges, as if someone had held it over a candle to make it look really old. I began reading aloud:

In the year of our Lord, 1664, I, Thomas Kitesprocket, was just fifteen years of age and already three years before the mast as a cabin boy aboard the H.M.S. Irritable, when the events I am about to recount came to pass. We were nearing the end of what had been a blessedly uneventful passage when our lookout cried, 'Ship ho!' Rushing to the rails, I spied a two-masted sloop flying His Majesty's colors, cleaving the waves and closing on us at full sail. Imagine my horror when I saw the beloved colors of our Royal Navy ensign lowered and replaced by a black flag with a white skull and crossbones - the Jolly Roger. We were being attacked by pirates!

Personally, I was riveted. Grandma Jo gently interrupted me, however, and pointed, "You seem to be losing your audience."

Looking over, I could see that Amy and Billy were not paying the least attention and had become engaged in running around in circles, pretending to be airplanes. I was surprised and, if I am honest, a little disappointed that they had so little interest in the spine-tingling narrative that I so fortuitously held in my quaking hands. Oh well. I jumped to the end:

> . . . and so, you, whoever so findeth this, my humble missive, follow well my indications, and you will enjoy riches beyond your wildest imagination.

"Look, Amy and Billy, there's a treasure map." *That* got their attention.

There was indeed a crude map drawn on the back of the letter, which I held out for inspection.

Billy began jumping up and down. "We have to find the x! We have to find the x!"

Although only four, he was onto something, as the map did, in fact, indicate that the object of our quest was marked by an "x." Our first step was to locate a large board protruding vertically from the sand, which, miraculously, after 332 years, was only yards from where benevolent providence had placed Thomas Kitesprocket's ancient epistle into our hands. From this starting point, we were instructed to count off paces, first in this direction, then in that, until, after two or three minutes of loud counting and vigorous pacing to and fro, we stood sweaty and panting where, indubitably, "x marks the spot." Two curious faces looked up at me, waiting expectantly.

I spelled it out for them, "We found the x, now start digging!"

In a flash, they were on their knees, scooping out sand with both hands. After they had dug without result to what I perceived to be the depth at which young Thomas would have buried his treasure,

I took careful, measured stock of the various landmarks around us and suggested that they dig about two feet to the left.

Billy hit pay dirt first. A silvery blade came into view. As they both worked feverishly, two crossed swords emerged into the light.

Billy was ecstatic, "A sword!" he proclaimed proudly, leaping to his feet and raising it above his head. "A toy one," he added, no doubt to ensure that no hovering adult felt the need to yank it out of his jubilant little hand.

Amy jumped up. "Another sword!" she yelled, and soon a full-fledged sword fight was underway.

"Hey," I interrupted, "what about the rest of the treasure? I bet there's more." Resuming the dig, six inches deeper, our two eager excavators uncovered the treasure chest itself. Although over three hundred years old, the thing it most resembled was a plastic shoebox like you might find at Peebles or Target. It seems that our young British sailor of yore had carefully selected the container that would best keep moisture from seeping into the booty.

Ripping off the lid, Billy surveyed the splendiferous plethora of riches and began recounting aloud, "There's toys, and rings, and CANDY!"

Flush with victory, their cheeks bulging with Hershey's kisses, our intrepid treasure hunters began dancing and chanting, "We're rich! We're rich!" as the rays of the setting sun drew azure- and-magenta streaks across the sky reflected below on the still waters of the glass-smooth bay.

So ended the most exciting day of their young lives.

Now, you might think that finding buried pirate treasure is a rare thing—like winning the lottery or being struck by lightning—and that once done, it would be nigh on impossible that you should ever be so fortunate as to stumble onto a second hoard. And, for ordinary folks, you'd be spot on; but I seem to be blessed with the knack. The very next year, during our vacation together in our new condo on Lewes Beach, Amy and Billy found another treasure map. This map was not drawn by Thomas Kitesprocket. In fact, we don't know who drew it, as there was no wordy and boring prologue. It is worth noting that whoever made this map did not include a lot of precise pacing, which can be prone to error. No, this map was a proper map showing landmarks.

We started on the beach, proceeded to the trash barrel, then on to the pole. A few landmarks later, we ended by counting houses, and you'll never believe this, but the treasure was buried in the sand in the breezeway under our very house. While nothing would ever match the excitement of that first "Eureka!" it was still very exciting that we had found another cache of fabulous riches. A swashbuckling time was had by all.

The year of our Lord, 1998, was an exciting one. A blue-and-brown, three-masted ship appeared one day, sailing the bay in front of our condo. I recognized it immediately as an armed merchant vessel known as a Dutch Pinnace. Through my spyglass, I could just make out the name on the stern, "Kalmar Nyckel"—no doubt it had been seized by pirates who had abandoned their ship in favor of this much newer one. Billy and I speculated that those pirates might row ashore any night to bury treasure. In fact, maybe they already had.

The next day, we formed a search party, and sure enough, we found a treasure map. Billy was just as excited as ever. Amy, however, now nine, did not seem as happy about the whole expedition. In fact, she stopped dead in her tracks, folded her arms, and said that she didn't think pirates had made the map at all.

As Billy trotted happily ahead, I gently pointed out to her that as a grown-up girl of nine, it was only reasonable that she might begin to question the existence of pirates. I confessed that I, myself, was a bit skeptical. "However," I said, "Billy is so happy thinking about the pirates. Is it more fun to believe that someone else made the map, or that pirates made the map?"

"Oh, it's a lot more fun to believe that pirates made the map," she said with a wide grin. Firm now in our shared belief in pirates, we resumed our quest and soon found a cache of freshly buried pirate treasure.

* * * * *

As the dunes shift, so do our lives. My dear wife, Carolyn, died in 2001, and for a few years, it was just me manning the fort in Lewes against pirates. Amy and Billy had moved on to other pursuits, but Billy suspected we might find a treasure map one weekend when a work colleague and her four-year-old daughter were visiting, and sure enough, we did. My brother Dave's son Will found pirate treasure when he was only three years old, a new record. My friends Ray and Kati invited me to spend time with them during their beach vacation, and their kids, Bekka and Greg, found buried pirate treasure in Cape May.

My last encounter with pirates was ten years ago. Now happily remarried, I spent a week with wife Michelle and two of her friends and their families in Nags Head, North Carolina.

During the week, I entertained the children with tales of Blackbeard, a pirate who famously prowled the Outer Banks. You're not going to believe this, but toward the end of the week, we found a treasure map written in Blackbeard's own hand, and this time, I really did have to lunge into crashing surf.

Blackbeard was even more straightforward than our anonymous Lewes pirate. He had made a detailed sketch of the entire beach and the road leading from it with the precise number of houses, each of the correct color. As we excitedly made our way from the beach in the direction indicated (the backyard of the house we were renting), I did not need to worry about the teenaged Jordan. I had explained to him about how I tended to find pirates wherever I went, and he was on board. I was a bit worried about ten-year-old Matt, but he was over the moon with excitement and even suggested that we call the local TV station so they could do a report on our search.

It was Christopher, a precocious boy of eight, who observed sardonically, "I don't think these houses were here hundreds of years ago, and I definitely don't think pirates used colored pencils." After a quick one-on-one pow-wow, he agreed that the kinds of pirates we were tracking did, in fact, use colored pencils. He also agreed that he didn't need to make any more insightful observations, as they might ruin the fun for the younger kids, and soon the little girls in the party had festooned themselves with the many rings, bracelets, necklaces, and tiaras that made up a significant portion of Blackbeard's treasure.

Tales of treasure have been recounted from time to time over the years by my adventurous, young companions, but that was the last of the great treasure hunts.

In my vast treasure hunting experience, I have learned three important lessons that, dear reader, I am now entrusting into your capable hands. First, it is important to know your different types of pirates. You must think carefully about what kind of treasure each is likely to bury so that you can find the map that will lead your young cohorts to the untold riches they are going to be most excited to find. Second, your chances of finding a treasure map are greatly increased if you make one. My final piece of advice—and this is key—is that you will only find buried treasure if you pay close attention to where you bury it.

Alas, time marches on apace. Little Billy is twenty-five. Little Amy is a maid of twenty-eight and soon to be a bride. Michelle and I can still be found in Lewes. As we stroll the shore or recline serenely by the water, our thoughts oft' harken back to those salad days when we marched in the ancient footsteps of pirates, young swashbucklers in tow, searching for buried treasure. Did I mention that Amy is getting married in October? I'm thinking that pirates will, once again, be beaching their skiffs on the sandy shores of Lewes and burying their swag by the light of the full moon in, shall we say, five or six years? In fact, my sources in the pirate underground tell me that planning has already begun.

I can hardly wait.

DOUG HARRELL IS ALMOST A NATIVE OF WILMINGTON, HAVING ARRIVED AT THE TENDER AGE OF FIVE. HE RECEIVED A BS FROM THE UNIVERSITY OF DELAWARE, AND A PH.D. FROM THE UNIVERSITY OF PENNSYLVANIA, BOTH IN CHEMICAL ENGINEERING. HIS CAREER IN THE PLASTICS INDUSTRY COVERED MORE THAN THIRTY YEARS, MOSTLY IN WILMINGTON, A BIT IN NEW JERSEY, AND A NON-CHARACTERISTIC, FAR-FLUNG STINT IN FERRARA, ITALY. ALL ALONG, HE HAS BEEN AN ENTHUSIASTIC WRITER MANQUÉ. ALTHOUGH HE HAS PUT OUT A SHORT MEMOIR PIECE AT CHRISTMAS FOR FRIENDS AND FAMILY FOR MANY YEARS, HE HAS PRIMARILY BEEN OCCUPIED IN NOT WRITING NUMEROUS MYSTERY SHORT STORIES AND A CHILDREN'S TIME-TRAVEL NOVEL. HE *IS* CURRENTLY WRITING A HISTORICAL NOVEL ABOUT THE LINDBERGH BABY KIDNAPPING OF THE 1930S. HIS FAVORITE WRITING SPOT IS PILOT POINT ON LEWES BEACH. HE GRATEFULLY ACKNOWLEDGES THE ENCOURAGEMENT OF HIS WIFE, MICHELLE, AND HER COUSIN, JEANIE BLAIR, TO FINALLY GET SERIOUS.

The Sweet Truth

By Jeanie P. Blair

Being up before dawn is worth it when you get to watch the sun rise over the ocean. Tenley Malloy finished her walk just as the bright fireball began ascending the horizon. She chose a spot on the sand, sat down, and inhaled deeply. The sunlight on her face, the salty scent of the ocean, and the swish of its surf far surpassed any spa treatments she'd ever overpaid for. She sipped from her water bottle and checked her watch—almost time to head home and get ready for her day at the bakery.

* * * * *

Moving to Rehoboth Beach and taking a job at Seaside Sweets was the best decision Tenley had ever made—that, and escaping the controlling grip of her father. One of Philadelphia's wealthiest financiers, Emmett Malloy gave no "follow your dreams" speeches to his children. The only option acceptable to him was to join the family business. Seduced by dollar signs, her older siblings gladly followed in Daddy Dearest's footsteps, while Tenley preferred spending her time cooking and baking with her mother and her fraternal grandmother, Blanche. Only once had she made the mistake of informing her father of her desire to forego the Ivy League for culinary school. She had never seen him so incensed, so off she went—unwillingly—to Princeton. Fortunately, Blanche secretly had another plan for her granddaughter. When Tenley graduated, Blanche handed her a gift box containing a generous check, a key to her Rehoboth Beach home, and a copy of the deed naming Tenley as co-owner. Tenley loved the

Hickman Street house, and Blanche knew the rental income from its two apartments would give her granddaughter the means to pursue her passion—without interference from her overbearing father.

*****

When Tenley arrived at the bakery, her partner was already there. "G'morning, Mae! How are you?"

The elder woman smiled. "Well hello, sugar. How're you?"

"Great, thanks," Tenley said, cinching an apron around her waist.

Mae was a sweet—but feisty—Southern grandma who reminded Tenley a lot of Blanche. When Tenley moved to Rehoboth and started working at Seaside Sweets, Mae took her under her wing and showed her the ropes of the bakery business. Several years later, Mae decided that being the sole proprietor was becoming too taxing for her, and she offered Tenley a partnership.

After they filled the display cases, Mae returned to the kitchen and Tenley took her place behind the counter. As she stooped to inventory the bakery boxes and bags, the doorbells clanged. She stood up and nearly gasped as she peered into the turquoise-blue eyes of her first customer. The striking stranger flashed a perfect grin—flanked by dimples as deep as the Atlantic.

"Good morning."

Damn. His husky voice gave her goose bumps. "Uh . . ." *Chill out, Tenley.* "Good morning. What can I get for you?"

"Hmm . . ." He eyed her up and down. "*Everything* back there looks delicious. What do you recommend?"

Tenley felt her cheeks flush. "The cranberry-orange scones are my favorite."

"Then I'll take one of those and a large, black coffee, please."

"Great," she said. As she filled his order, she couldn't help but sneak glances of him, praying she wouldn't get caught. He was tall, and under his button-down shirt, he was conspicuously muscular. She imagined combing her fingers through his thick, black hair. Tenley placed his order on the counter. "That'll be six-fifty, please."

He handed her a ten-dollar bill. "Thanks. Keep the change."

"Thank you," she said. "Have a great day."

"You, too." He turned to leave, but paused and turned back. "Uh . . . would you happen to know of any rooms or apartments for rent?"

"Well, actually, yes," she said. "I have a house with two furnished apartments, and one's available. It's several blocks off the Avenue, so it's nice and quiet."

"Sounds great," he said. "When can I see it?"

"Any evening," she said.

"How 'bout tonight?"

"Tonight's fine." Her heart raced. "Seven o'clock?"

"Seven's good."

"Great." She wrote her name and address on an order ticket and handed it to him. "See you then." As he walked toward the exit, she called out to him. "Wait! I didn't catch your name."

He turned around. "Dalton. Dalton Lynch." He looked at the order ticket. "See you tonight, Tenley Malloy."

The rest of her day dragged. Thankfully, she arrived home with just enough time to shower before Dalton arrived. She wrapped her damp, blonde hair into a loose bun and slid into a pair of denim shorts and a striped tank top. She threw on a bracelet and earrings, and swiped on some eyeliner and lip gloss before heading up to the rental.

* * * * *

Dalton mentally reviewed his assignment as he drove toward Hickman Street. During their last conversation, Emmett Malloy made it perfectly clear that he would no longer tolerate his daughter's defiance. He was never able to fully infiltrate her alliance with his wife or his mother, so all he knew for sure was that Tenley was living at his mother's beach house and working in a local bakery. He had fully expected that she'd fail on her own and would return home in a matter of months, begging him for a job. But several years later, she was still beyond his reach, and his need to regain control of her had become an obsession. He instructed Dalton to find out exactly what she was up to so that he could devise a plan to get her back. But Dalton Lynch was not prepared for the likes of Tenley Malloy. It didn't help that Emmett hadn't seen his daughter in years. From her father's description, Dalton was expecting to see a skinny, ordinary-looking girl. He hadn't anticipated a stunning, green-eyed woman with the body of an Olympic swimmer. He was usually willing to do anything to impress his boss, but having met her, he was strangely uneasy about his assignment.

Closing the door of his BMW, he surveyed the dwelling before him. Another surprise. He had pictured a dilapidated shack that would make the Munster's house look palatial—not this pristine, gray, two-story a mere four lots from the beach, adorned with a white balcony on each floor and a rooftop deck that likely offered spectacular views. Emmett Malloy had obviously underestimated his daughter.

* * * * *

Tenley heard a car door slam and peeked out the window. There stood Dalton Lynch, wearing a pair of navy basketball shorts and a gray Yale T-shirt, which confirmed her assumption of what was beneath the button-down he'd worn earlier. Her pulse quickened as she stepped out onto the deck. "Dalton, up here!"

Dalton took the stairs to the second level. "Beautiful place you've got here."

"Thanks." She gestured toward the door. "After you."

Dalton's tour ended in the kitchen, where he and Tenley discussed the rental details. "Perfect," he said. "I appreciate the month-to-month option. When can I move in?"

"Right away, if you'd like."

"Excellent. I'll move in tomorrow."

"Great. Here's your key." She handed him the key ring and started for the door.

"Tenley . . . have you had dinner yet?"

"Actually, no," she answered.

"I'm going to Dogfish if you'd like to join me."

Didn't see that coming. "Uh . . . okay. Just let me grab my purse."

"Great. I'll wait in the car," he said.

* * * * *

Fortunately, the line wasn't too long, so they were seated quickly and placed their orders. A friendly waitress delivered their drinks.

"So what brought you to Rehoboth?" Tenley asked.

"I work for a developer. I'm looking at properties that might become available soon."

"How long do you think you'll be here?"

"Not really sure."

She nodded.

While they ate, Tenley found herself attempting to field Dalton's rapid-fire questions. She fidgeted when the discussion began to feel more like an interrogation than a casual conversation.

As they finished their dinner, Tenley looked at her watch. "Wow. It's late, and I have an early day tomorrow."

"Yeah, me, too," he said. They both reached for the check, and his hand covered hers. "I've got this."

"No. I should be treating my new tenant."

"Not necessary. Besides, *I* invited *you,* remember?"

Tenley conceded and attempted to withdraw her hand, but his grip tightened. She was relieved when the waitress arrived for the bill and diverted his attention.

*****

The drive back was quiet. Dalton sensed Tenley's unease and feared he had asked too many questions. When they arrived at her house, Tenley thanked him for dinner, exited the car, and then strode up to her door. Dalton waited until she was safely inside, then drove away.

*****

The next day, there was a steady stream of bakery patrons. Tenley had hoped Dalton would be among them, but no such luck. When her shift ended, she went home and had a light dinner. As she rinsed off her dish, a knock on the door startled her. She dried her hands and went to answer it. There stood Dalton, holding a small brown box.

"A package for you, Ms. Malloy. I intercepted the delivery guy and figured I'd hand-deliver it to you."

"Oh, thanks." She paused. "Hey, I was about to have some wine on the roof deck. Wanna join me?"

He swiped his brow. "Well, I'm kinda sweaty from the move—"

"Sunset's an hour away, so you still have time for a shower."

"Okay. But only if you let me bring the wine."

"Deal," she said. "I'll grab some glasses and an opener and meet you up there."

Dalton arrived with a chilled bottle of sparkling Moscato. He popped the cork and filled both glasses, then took in the view. "Wow. This is amazing. I'm from Pittsburgh—I only saw a beach twice as a kid when we visited some relatives in New Jersey."

"What a shame," she said. "It's very therapeutic. No matter how down I am, this fixes everything."

"I'm sure," he said.

Tenley shared stories of her family's vacations in Rehoboth. Dalton was so easy to talk to. She found herself sharing more with him than she'd intended, stopping short of rehashing the drama with her father.

The sunset was magnificent—streaks of yellow and orange were like watercolor brushstrokes across the violet sky.

"Doesn't get more beautiful than this," she said with a sigh.

"It's breathtaking," Dalton said, though Tenley noticed he was looking at her, not the sky.

She locked eyes with him and was certain she'd stopped breathing. *Snap out of it.* "Uh . . . more wine?"

"Sure." He held up his glass.

Tenley tipped the bottle, but only a few drops trickled out. "Oops. Maybe we'd better call it a night?"

"Looks that way," Dalton said with a laugh. "This was great, but I hope I didn't keep you up too late."

"Actually, no. I'm off tomorrow."

"Me, too," he said. "Hey, maybe you could show me around? Unless you have other plans."

"No. I'd be happy to."

"Cool!" Dalton grabbed the empty glasses. "I'll walk you down."

"Oh, no, that's okay."

"C'mon, I insist."

She smiled and followed him down to her porch. She took hold of the glasses, but Dalton didn't let go. He pulled them—and her—closer. His gaze met hers, and he leaned in and kissed her softly.

"Good night." He released the glasses. "See you tomorrow."

Tenley's lips were momentarily paralyzed. "Good . . . night."

Once inside, she locked her door and took a deep breath. *That had to be the wine.*

*****

They spent most of the next day in Lewes. When they passed the ferry terminal, Dalton made her promise him a ride sometime. The day went better than Tenley expected. She feared things might be awkward, but Dalton acted as if nothing had happened the night before. When they returned, they parted ways with a quick hug. Oddly, Tenley was both relieved *and* disappointed. *Yep—must've been the wine.*

*****

During the next few weeks, the two spent more and more time together. Dalton even began visiting the bakery to spend her breaks with her. He seemed intent on keeping things casual between them, so Tenley tried to forget about their kiss. She couldn't deny her feelings for him, but wouldn't risk losing his friendship.

"Everything okay, sugar?" Mae asked.

Tenley snapped out of her trance. "Sorry, Mae. Just preoccupied."

"Thinkin' 'bout that handsome fella, huh?"

"Oh, no," Tenley lied.

Mae smirked. "I wasn't born yesterday. You're crazy about him, aren't you?"

Tenley frowned. She never could fool Mae. "It doesn't matter. He doesn't feel the same."

Mae shook her head. "Oh, honey, you're wrong. That boy's in love."

"What? No way!"

"Oh yes," Mae answered. "That's the sweet truth. He can't peel his eyes off you for a second. He looks at you like he wants to sop you up with a biscuit." She let out a jolly laugh.

The bells chimed and in walked Dalton. Mae said hello to him, then winked at Tenley and headed for the kitchen. He stopped, looked at Mae, and then at Tenley. "I'm sorry, did I interrupt something?"

"Nah. Just shop talk," Tenley lied.

"Ah."

"Hey, I just heard that my favorite band is going to play on the ferry," Tenley said. "We could finally take that cruise I promised you."

"Cool! When?"

"Saturday night. My treat."

"Only if I buy the drinks."

"Deal. You're quite the negotiator, Mr. Lynch."

Dalton laughed. "You're not so bad yourself, Ms. Malloy."

* * * * *

Dalton imagined it was a perfect evening to be on the water—clear skies and a comfy seventy degrees. The evening sunset on the bay would be magnificent. Tenley purchased their tickets, and the pair boarded the vessel. They stopped by the bar for drinks before taking their seats.

"This is so cool," Dalton said. "I've never been on a ferry."

"Really? It's fun. And there's no better place to watch the sun set."

The band played a good mix of classic rock and pop. After the set, Tenley shared the history of Cape Henlopen and its lighthouses. The sunset was breathtaking, but the temperature dipped rapidly. Tenley twitched. Assuming she'd caught a chill, Dalton draped his hoodie over her shoulders and wrapped his arm around her.

"Thanks," she said, "but aren't you cold?"

"Nah, I'm good." The warmth of her against him was all he needed.

Tenley began telling Dalton how she ended up in Rehoboth, and what a controlling bully her father had been. He was stunned by the horrible things he was hearing about his boss, but he knew Tenley was telling the truth. The only thing she was guilty of was wanting to live her life on her own terms, and she deserved that.

"He just can't stand that I made it on my own."

"Sounds like it."

Tenley paused and took a deep breath. "Wow."

"What?"

"I've never shared that with anyone but Mae." She rested her head on his shoulder. "You're a good friend, Dalton Lynch."

If she only knew. A feeling of dread overcame Dalton. If Tenley knew the truth, she'd be devastated. How could he keep this up? He realized he was no better than the lying scum he worked for. *Game over. This ends now.* He'd lose his job, but that didn't matter. Losing her would be far worse. Though he feared she'd never forgive him, he had to come clean. He owed her that much. But now was not the time. He didn't want to ruin this beautiful evening with her, certain it would be their last.

On the drive home, Tenley recapped their day, but Dalton struggled to engage. He was content just to see her so happy—probably the happiest he'd ever seen her—which made him loathe himself even more.

"Dalton, are you listening?"

He snapped back to reality. "I'm sorry. What?"

"I asked if you liked the band."

"Oh yeah. They were great," he said, trying to sound enthusiastic.

"Cool. Maybe we can see them again soon."

He forced a smile. "That would be nice."

They pulled into the driveway and got out of the car. Dalton walked Tenley to her door, and thanked her again for a great evening.

"Are you okay?" she asked.

"Yeah. Just tired."

"Well, get some rest. I'm off again tomorrow if you want to do something."

He paused. "How 'bout a walk on the beach in the morning?"

"Sure. You know I'm up early, so come down whenever you're ready," she said.

"Will do." He pulled her in for a hug. Dalton closed his eyes and lingered longer than normal, knowing this would be the last time he'd hold her. He needed to savor every second—the feel of her against him, the scents of her shampoo and perfume, the warmth of her breath on his neck. Every. Last. Detail. It took all his strength to let her go. Though he knew it was wrong, he took her face in his hands and drew her lips to his. When they parted, Dalton stared into her eyes. "Good night, Tenley."

* * * * *

To Tenley's dismay, she'd been up since dawn, yet was amazed she'd slept at all. Several hours had passed, and she prayed Dalton would arrive soon. She was trying to relax with a cup of coffee when she spotted his hoodie at the other end of the sofa. She grabbed it and held it close. It still smelled of his cologne. Tenley closed her eyes and could feel his soft lips on hers and his strong arms around her again. Her heart raced. She had no idea when things had shifted. The thought of scaring him away was terrifying, but she'd have to broach the subject.

* * * * *

Dalton stood in front of Tenley's door, forcing himself to breathe. *Moment of truth.* He would tell her everything, including—*for what it was worth*—how he felt about her. He swallowed hard and knocked. The door swung open like she'd been standing right there, waiting.

"Good morning," she said.

"Hey." He smiled, fighting his angst. "Sorry I'm so late."

"No problem." She handed him his hoodie. "It's chilly. You should wear this."

"Thanks," he said, and pulled it over his head.

"Thank *you* for letting me borrow it."

"You're welcome." He stepped aside. "Ready?"

"Yep." She tucked her cell phone and keys into her jacket pocket and took a blanket from the chair by the door. "Just in case we want to sit."

"Good idea." Based on her cheerfulness, he gathered she was expecting the "relationship" chat and had no idea she was about to be blindsided. *Dammit.* He hated himself.

The two made small talk until they reached the surf's edge, then Dalton took the blanket from Tenley. *Why prolong the agony—for either of them.* "How 'bout if we sit first."

"Okay," she said.

They spread the blanket across the sand and sat facing each other. "Tenley, there's something I need to tell you." A stabbing pain pierced his chest.

She looked confused. "What is it, Dalton—what's wrong?" She'd obviously caught his pained expression.

"Tenley, I—" Her cell phone rang.

"I'm sorry. It's my grandmother. I'll just be a second." She tapped the screen and held it to her ear. "Hi, Grandma." She listened intently, with a perplexed look on her face that quickly turned to shock. "Oh. My. God. What? But why?" She sprung from the blanket and glared at Dalton, tears welling up in her eyes.

Shit—she knows. Dalton jumped up and reached for her. "Tenley—" She turned her back on him.

"Grandma, I have to go." She started crying. "I'll be okay. I'll call you later." She whipped around to face Dalton. "You bastard." She darted toward Hickman Street.

"Tenley, wait! Let me explain!" He chased her down and jumped in front of her. She tried to sidestep him, but he gripped her shoulders.

"Wait? Wait for what? More lies?" She sobbed. "All this time. It was all bullshit."

"No! I swear to you, it wasn't." He closed his eyes and shook his head.

"Not all of it. Your father sent me here to spy on you, *that's* true. But he made you out to be this ungrateful brat who betrayed him. He played me, Tenley. And I knew it the moment I met you."

"Then why did you do this?"

"Because I had to be sure. I didn't count on any of this. I wasn't supposed to . . ."

"You weren't supposed to *what*, Dalton?"

"I wasn't supposed to get involved. I wasn't supposed to fall in love with you."

* * * * *

Angry and hurt as she was, Tenley knew he was telling the truth. The whole thing reeked of her father. She always knew he'd never rest until he won.

"Please. You *have* to believe me," Dalton pleaded. "The reason I was so late today is because I called Emmett. I told him it was over, and that I was going to tell you everything." He wiped her tears. "I'm so sorry, Tenley." The remorse in his eyes was real.

Tenley punched his chest. "I hate you, you know."

"I know." Dalton panted, pressing his lips to her forehead. "I hate me more."

They held each other tightly, then Tenley pulled back. "So I guess this means you're unemployed now."

"Guess so. Do you think my landlord will cut me some slack till I find a job?"

"Maybe." She shrugged. "Hey—I hear there's a bakery in town that's looking for a CFO."

"Really?" He smiled.

"Yep. And I know the owner. I could put in a good word for you."

He pulled her in for a lingering kiss. "I love you so much, Tenley Malloy."

"I love you, too, Dalton Lynch," she said. "And that's the sweet truth."

A NATIVE DELAWAREAN, JEANIE PITRIZZI BLAIR RESIDES IN NEWARK WITH HER HUSBAND, SAM, AND THEIR MINIATURE SCHNAUZERS, SCHATZIE AND BELLA. SHE HAS POSSESSED A LOVE FOR READING, WRITING, AND THE ENGLISH LANGUAGE SINCE SHE WAS A CHILD, WHICH SHE LARGELY ATTRIBUTES TO HER GRADE-SCHOOL ENGLISH TEACHERS. JEANIE'S FIRST PUBLISHED PIECE WAS A POEM THAT SHE ENTERED IN A NATIONAL POETRY CONTEST. THIS IS HER THIRD SHORT STORY PUBLISHED IN THE REHOBOTH BEACH READS ANTHOLOGIES. HER FIRST, "SOMEWHERE BETWEEN CRAB CAKES AND COCKTAILS," APPEARED IN *BEACH DAYS*, AND HER SECOND, "MERMAID'S MOON," WAS FEATURED IN LAST YEAR'S *BEACH NIGHTS*. THOUGH SHE WORKS FULL-TIME AS AN OFFICE ADMINISTRATOR, JEANIE CONTINUES TO PURSUE HER DREAM OF BECOMING A SUCCESSFUL ROMANCE NOVELIST. SHE HAS SPENT HER WHOLE LIFE VACATIONING AT THE BEACH—HER MOST FAVORITE PLACE AND THE INSPIRATION AND SETTING FOR MANY OF HER STORIES—AND GREATLY ENJOYS SPENDING TIME WITH HER FAMILY IN LONG NECK, DELAWARE. JEANIE WOULD LIKE TO THANK HER DEAR FAMILY AND FRIENDS FOR THEIR CONTINUED SUPPORT AND ENCOURAGEMENT.

A Day in the Life

By David Strauss

It wasn't supposed to be like this. His first day off in ten days and it's overcast and chilly, a northeast wind blowing sand and whipping up waves into frenzied whitecaps like frosting, the sun held captive behind a wall of gunmetal-gray clouds, hanging silent and ominous over the empty beach. Johnny watches the ocean. Maybe he'll salvage the day with a little surf session, but even the lineup is empty this morning, the break too disorganized and choppy for anything worthwhile, so he exhales loudly and turns away, pulling the hoodie over his head, trudging home. *Sunny and warm for over two weeks straight and my one fucking day off, I can't even go to the beach.*

Johnny walks west along Rehoboth Avenue, past Kohr Brothers and Sunsations, crosses over First Street, head down, flip-flops slapping loudly against unforgiving pavement. The smell of fresh coffee hits him at the Sea Shell Shop, and he follows it to its source at Browseabout Books, ducks inside, and orders a large cup of house blend with cream and sugar. He turns to leave, sees those heavy clouds looming low outside the window, and decides to loiter awhile in the bookstore, window-shopping book covers and looking at toys.

Billy and Steph slept in this morning, many beers at Dogfish Head and some late night shooters at Summer House, rediscovering the joys of pushing tomorrow further away, trying to recapture those youthful summers when they lived and worked in this resort town. But what seemed like a good idea in the wee hours is turning out to be a mistake—incessant throb-throb-throbbing of pain pulsing from the temples to the center of the forehead, again, again, again—you can't go back, you can never go back.

Billy rises first, face bloated and wrinkled, body screaming at brain—*I thought you knew better; you told yourself never again*—but he's in no mood for it this morning, so he stumbles to the bathroom for a warm shower and a bottle of aspirin. Steph rolls herself deeper beneath the covers, trying to hide from the hangover, but it's no use and so she, too, rises from the dead and begins to work on making herself feel normal again, to feel human.

"Coffee, Billy," she mumbles, her throat dry and raspy, "we need to find us some coffee."

Zlata, in her white shorts and white top, cheap white sneakers and stained white socks, stands behind the white counter of Kohr Brothers, watching the little activity on the boardwalk, the birds fighting against a strong northeasterly breeze, the sea oats standing sideways, wishing she'd remembered to bring her sweatshirt. *The photographs on the website never showed Rehoboth like this. Where is the warmth, the sun? I can get this back in Ukraine.*

Her best friend, Anna, her schoolmate back home, zips her own sweatshirt up tight, hugs herself, and shivers against the chill. "Why don't you just go buy another sweatshirt?"

Zlata considers the question, then does the math—twenty bucks for a cheaply made sweatshirt when she's already got two perfectly good ones back at the apartment. "No, no, I'll be all right. You know we're saving our money so we can tour America. I want to have all I can by September for holiday." The girls turn and begin the daily task of wiping down stainless steel, wiping down sticky countertops, and waiting for customers who most likely won't come, backs braced against the summer chill.

Billy and Steph are dressed and out, walking gingerly along Rehoboth Avenue toward the beach. "Maybe," he says, "maybe the ocean breeze will do our heads some good."

Steph looks doubtfully at the gray sky and mumbles, "Unless that sea breeze is caffeinated, I doubt it. Coffee, Billy. I need some coffee."

The pair makes the short trek along the boardwalk from the south side of Rehoboth Avenue to the north, strolling hand in hand past Dolles and then Kohr Brothers, Billy pausing to look at the daily selections, considering a little soft-serve for a late breakfast.

"C'mon. Ice cream later. We're stopping at the first place that sells coffee." Steph pulls Billy up Rehoboth Avenue, mind set on only one thing, the intoxicating aroma of freshly brewed coffee drawing her into the front door of Browseabout Books.

"Are you sure about this, Dad?"

Greg leans forward, glances out the front windshield of his car, zipping south along Route One, just north of Dover. The skies are gray, the landscape socked in with clouds, late summer morning looking more like dusk, perhaps a day better spent inside a movie theater or a museum, not an afternoon trip to the beach. He smiles at his son slumped in the passenger's seat, the boy's face full of doubt, "Yep. Just wait until we get to Rehoboth. The sun always shines at the beach. It'll be fine."

The boy looks out his window, watches flat fields pass by, thick clouds swirling overhead. "I don't know about this, Dad."

Johnny is cross-legged on the floor of the bookstore, shelves rising like canyon walls around him and he's trapped inside now, books scattered all around, one spread open in his lap. The surfer is enthralled with the stories of the concrete towers, how on a clear day visitors atop the Cape Henlopen tower can see almost fifteen miles of coastal Delaware. He flips a page, examines an old black-and-white photograph, the caption reading: "Soldiers monitor our coastlines during World War II as they search for approaching enemy ships or Nazi submarines." He sips from his second cup of coffee and turns another page, his mind lost in time.

"Outlets? Really?" Billy is still thinking about ice cream, but Steph has other ideas and so he follows along dutifully. It had been one of the items on her list of things to do; it's just that he wasn't really ready for it, not this early in the week.

Steph has her cup of coffee and is moving faster now, eyes on the prize, looking forward to a day spent shopping. Billy, on the other hand, knows he'll spend most of his time following her around while she tries on clothes or browses from store to store, him carrying her purchases back to the car, all the while cursing himself for forgetting his golf clubs.

"Can I at least pick where we get to eat lunch?"

Steph is opening the car door and pauses to look up at her husband. "As long as it's not too far from the outlets, then sure." As they slide into their seats, she adds an addendum. "But only after I get some shopping done."

Billy buckles in and stares up at the dark sky. "If the sun comes out, I want to get to the beach today."

His wife smiles. "I promise. If the sun comes out, we'll leave the outlets and come back to the beach." She giggles. "I'll even buy you an ice cream."

Zlata and Anna lean across the counter, watching Rehoboth, bored. Three young boys, sporting identical swim trunks, surf shirts, and water shoes, hurry along excitedly, yammering loudly back and forth. They each pause for a second in front of the ice cream counter, but before any of them can utter a sound, Dad's voice booms from behind them, "No ice cream. Maybe later, if the sun comes out."

The boys look at each other and shrug, running down to the boardwalk. They turn and wait for Mom and Dad, a good twenty yards behind, reluctant partners on this expedition, the voices of their three children urging them to hurry up.

Zlata turns away, plastic spoon in hand, pulls the silver lever on the soft-serve machine, a small zebra swirl spilling into the tiny spoon's bowl. She pops it in her mouth and moves on to the next machine, repeating the process down the line. "I'm going to get so fat if I keep eating like this."

Anna smiles. "Hand me a spoon, Z. We've got nothing better to do."

Greg is stuck in traffic by the outlets, always busy in the summer, but even more so when the weather is bad. The sky is still gray, but not as dark as it was back in Dover. The air is lighter, the flags alongside Route One ruffling lightly in the breeze, outside temperature gauge in his car showing seventy-nine, almost ten degrees warmer since the toll booth.

He rolls down the windows, sounds of cars starting and stopping, and a touch of fresh air filling the vehicle. The boy sits up, stares at the action on both sides of the road, parking lots jammed with cars, shoppers lugging purchases from store to store, a long line of cars trying to find spaces where, clearly, none can be found.

Greg looks at his son and smiles. "Must be giving something away over there."

"What about the sun, Dad? You said the sun would be out."

Greg smiles again. "Well, we're not at the beach yet. I said the sun always shines at the beach, right? So, technically. . . ."

"But, Dad, it's just down the road. We're almost there." He looks at the sky. "I don't see any sun, Dad."

Sometimes it's what we don't see.

While Johnny sat on the floor surrounded by books and Billy and Steph shopped, as Zlata and Anna ate ice cream and Greg and his son watched the world pass by from the seats of their car, the wind shifted. The flags in and around Rehoboth, which had been flying as if those cold northeasterly winds were trying to rip them from their poles, slowly spun, as the southern winds snuck back into town. Colorful canvas banners began to billow gently in the southern breeze.

At first, the dark-gray clouds became light-gray clouds. Gray gave way to white, and then as Billy steps out from yet another clothing store and Greg finally finishes fighting the traffic, making a left onto Rehoboth Avenue, as they inch along past Dogfish Head and down the blocks—4th, 3rd, 2nd—a patch of blue sky appears overhead.

Billy nudges Steph, points to the heavens, and nods. "Sun's coming out."

She replies curtly, "Not out yet."

Billy is smiling.

Zlata feels the warmth almost immediately, the change in the wind, softening of the day. She leans out over the counter, poking her head out like an animal emerging from hibernation, the sweet smells of summer returning. She looks over at Anna and smiles. "Be right back."

After circling the crowded Rehoboth neighborhoods a time or two, Greg finds a parking spot on Philadelphia Street and goes about unpacking the requisite beach day supplies. He hands his son a beach chair and a boogie board, drapes a striped towel over his shoulder, and puts a hat on the boy's head.

"Still no sun, Dad."

Greg glances up at the sky, mostly blue now, streaks of clouds overhead, drifting slowly to the north. "We're not at the beach, yet."

The child grunts a *hmmpff*, then turns and drags his boogie board along the sidewalk, slick bottom scraping rough concrete, Velcro strap wrapped around bony wrist, heading ever closer toward the sand. Dad trails behind, a beast of plastic burden—buckets and shovels and cooler and chair—a father and son on their own summer safari. They follow Delaware Avenue down to Funland, step out onto the boardwalk into the chaos of a moving current, people passing by in all directions while the child fights his way through, popping out the other side of the crowd into the glare of a bright summer sun reflecting off the surface of that endless Atlantic Ocean, soft, cotton-ball clouds floating lazily above the horizon, gulls crying out their welcome to the shore.

Dad passes through to the other side, the beach side, a big smile spreading across his face. "See, I told you the sun always shines at the beach."

The Ukranian girl, almost five thousand miles from home, sits on a white bench facing away from the beach, facing west, closes her eyes and inhales, the soft heat of an afternoon sun warming her face, the million smells of a summer day in downtown Rehoboth, the sounds of a city coming to life—kids and cars and crying gulls. *I can't get this back in Ukraine.*

Johnny stumbles blindly from the bookstore, spilling onto a sidewalk alive with movement, shielding bright light from squinting eyes, trying to adjust to his new reality. Johnny's got a book clutched in his hand and he turns, walking slowly toward the ocean, a very different day, a very different town, this time around. He finds his place in the back of the line at Kohr Brothers, mind set on an orange vanilla twist with chocolate sprinkles, watching three small boys in front of him eating their own cones, melted ice cream dripping off chins, circling their parents, content. A father and son are in front of him, the boy asking his dad, "Why does the sun always shine at the beach?", a couple behind him bickering, the woman complaining about shopping, the man laughing, "I'll even buy you an ice cream you said," Johnny unsure about the meaning of either conversation. The worker behind the counter is leaning out, screaming *Zlata, Zlata,* and Johnny watches as a girl on a white bench sits up and opens her eyes, hops off that bench, and walks briskly over to where they are. She ducks behind the counter and ties her apron, leans out, and calls, "Next!". Johnny steps up and orders his twist cone with chocolate sprinkles, smiles back at the cute girl, and walks to the boardwalk, occupying the same spot Zlata had just vacated.

And as the sunlight glitters across a dancing ocean and dolphins surface to the delight of tourists, couples walk, fingers intertwined—caramel popcorn or soft-serve—as they stroll along the boardwalk, Johnny sits enjoying his ice cream, his day off, his beach town. The cars and the buses and the people move, the gulls dip and cry above the action on the boardwalk, the sunbathers on the beach, and he knows that it's all some perfect, complex puzzle where every piece fits, where the problems of the world are a million miles away, if just for now, and that Johnny is truly blessed to be a part of this place, in this time, this beach life.

DAVID STRAUSS GREW UP VISITING THE BEACH, SPENDING HIS SUMMERS IN OCEAN CITY, MD, AND CLEARWATER BEACH, FL. HE SPENT HIS COLLEGE YEARS LIVING AND WORKING IN OCEAN CITY, WHERE HE DELIVERED PIZZAS ON HIS BICYCLE. DAVID HAS HAD POETRY AND/OR SHORT STORIES PUBLISHED IN *THE SCARAB, THE DAMOZEL, SELF X-PRESS, DIRT RAG MAGAZINE, THE BOARDWALK,* AND *BEACH NIGHTS.* HE HAS ALSO PUBLISHED TWO NOVELS, *DANGEROUS SHOREBREAK* AND *STRUCTURALLY DEFICIENT,* THROUGH CREATESPACE. HE TEACHES US HISTORY AND LIVES IN BEL AIR, MD, WITH HIS WIFE, MIRELLA, HIS SON, LIAM, AND HIS SLIGHTLY NEUROTIC DACHSHUND, BRAIDEN.

And the Sea Hath Spoken

By Darryl Forrest

"He called again," Kai said. She adjusted the hair clip holding her dreadlocks and continued folding white cotton bath towels freshly hatched from the dryer. The smell of Downy weaved in and out of the aroma of fresh biscuits that wafted in from the kitchen where Molly prepared morning breakfast for twenty-eight guests. Her bed and breakfast inn was running at full capacity, as it always did in the weeks following the Fourth of July, all the way through to the end of August.

"This is the second morning in a row," Molly said, in an agitated and fearful tone. The calls had come from Room 202, The Douglass House Room.

Molly had named the rooms after historic inns that once stood along the beach in Rehoboth: The Surf House Room, The Bright House Room, The Henlopen Room. She had gotten the idea after getting ownership of the building in the divorce proceedings.

The inn had been a vacation house belonging to her ex-husband that had been in his family for four generations. After he ran off with a young, blonde legal assistant in his DC law firm, she made a deal not to take him to the cleaners—she took the vacation house instead. She knew it pained him, but he was the one who had not made her sign a prenup, and she was angry her life had been turned upside down.

But she wasn't angry for long. Molly had a fondness for women that became more when she met Kai at a Rehoboth support group after her divorce. Kai was ten years younger and coming off a five-year relationship. It wasn't love at first sight, but over several outings they warmed up to each other over Fiona Apple and sloe gin fizzes. Lucky for Molly, not only was Kai a free spirit and a great kisser, she also had a degree in hotel management from the University of Delaware. They became lovers and business partners in the blink of an eye.

"Grab the mop and a bucket," Molly said. "Follow me; we need to put a stop to this." Molly retreated to the kitchen, where she removed the homemade biscuits—perfect in their flakiness and light-brown coloring—from the oven. Every day, she made time to enjoy a biscuit slathered in butter and local raspberry jam while she sipped from a cup of tea and read the local newspaper. Her favorite part was the crime section. She had a fascination with local debauchery.

She wasn't sure where the fascination came from. Maybe it was the house. It was built on the site of the old Douglass House. Back in the 1800s, a sickly minister from Delaware visited a religious camp on the Jersey shore and was restored to full health. He was so inspired by his return to health and the role he felt the camp played in it that he said "And the sea hath spoken" and made plans to build a religious encampment on the Delaware shore called Rehoboth. Alcohol and gambling were banned from the city, and the deplorables migrated to The Douglass House to drink, play cards, and hang with harlots. Molly noted the coincidence that they were knocking on the door of Room 202—The Douglass House Room. She didn't believe in coincidences.

Molly knocked, and the guest answered the door. Dr. Hobson, Molly remembered from the check-in screen. He was wearing an orange Izod shirt that made him look, well, like an orange. Molly liked the way the green alligator looked on his orange shirt. She was fond of stark color contrasts. It was one way that she and Kai were different. Kai never understood why Molly kept putting purple towels in the green guest bathrooms.

"Ladies," he said, as he attempted to straighten the wispy gray hair that was piled up on one side. A neatly trimmed goatee encircled his mouth, which consisted of fleshy lips and tobacco-stained teeth. Molly wondered whether he was trying to hide those imperfections. Molly and Kai entered the room with bucket and mop in tow. They noticed a young man sitting on the cream-colored couch that doubled as a daybed. Molly figured he wasn't more than twenty-five. She took in the short, blue velour shorts with white trim and a horizontal rainbow-striped tank top and noted that his hair was straight and cut like someone had placed a bowl on his head and cut around the edges. His features were soft—almost feminine—and his legs and arms were long, hairless, and tanned.

The young man hadn't been with the guest when he checked in the night before. Molly had Googled the older man earlier, which she often did to get to know her guests before they arrived, so she knew the man in 202 was Dr. Marlon Hobson, a professor and a resident scholar at The Council for Integrity in Science, a DC think tank. Molly had read one of his blogs out of curiosity and discovered he was a climate denier who wrote that measurements of CO_2 in the atmosphere were wrong. He said man-made climate change was a hoax—fake news.

"How can people live with their heads stuck in the sand?" Molly had asked Kai.

Molly walked by the orange fruit of a man with the mop in her hand. His companion was watching an old rerun of the late eighties TV show, *21 Jump Street*. He didn't seem to notice Molly and Kai as they walked behind him to get to the bathroom. Molly opened the door and noticed water pooled on the ceramic tiled floor. On a towel rack mounted on the wall next to the claw-foot tub, two white cotton guest towels soaked with water dripped onto the floor.

Molly threw the mop down on the floor. This was the second occurrence in as many days. She waded across the bathroom floor in her Crocs and ripped open the shower curtain that encased the claw-foot tub. She reached down to the hot and cold water handles and tried to twist them, but they were already turned off tightly. The bathtub was dry; likewise, the sink. Molly and Kai exchanged a look.

"I can assure you we didn't flood the bathroom," the man said. Which was exactly what he had said the previous day. Kai picked up the mop and started wiping up the water.

Molly sniffed. She hadn't noticed the odd smell before. It wasn't a sewage smell like a pipe was backed up or something, but rather a fishy smell—not bad fishy, more like the ocean. She smelled the towels. Seawater?

"Dr. Hobson, are you sure you didn't use these as beach towels?" Molly asked. "We specifically ask guests not to use the bath towels on the beach."

Kai shook her head as she mopped the remaining water from the floor. She examined the two wet towels and placed them in the bucket. No sign of sand. Grabbing the bucket, she headed out the door to get fresh towels.

"No, we did not, Ms. Jensen. Just like yesterday, I was making a blog entry in my computer at the desk over there, and Stanford was watching the idiot box like he's doing now. I went to use the water closet and, behold, just like yesterday, the bathroom is a swamp."

"But that doesn't make any sense." Molly held her index finger up to her lips, as if hoping a reasonable explanation would come to her.

"Perhaps it's something of the supernatural variety," the professor said, as Kai returned with the replacement towels.

"Yeah, right, *supernatural*," Kai said under her breath as she straightened the towels on the rack. "Didn't we go through this before?"

She was referring to the time a few years ago when an episode of *Ghost Finders* was filmed at the inn. There had been several incidents of spirit activity: a rocking chair on the third floor rocking by itself in the middle of the night, a claw-foot tub shaking while a guest was taking a bath, a shot glass from the lobby minibar found shattered on the wooden floor. The cast of the television show had staked out the inn on a cold, blustery winter's night. There were several dramatic "did you hear that" and "what was that" prompts, followed by looks of fear by the cast members. In the end, there were no great revelations of spirit activity. Molly thought it was good marketing despite the lack of evidence.

Kai didn't believe in ghosts; Molly wasn't sure. If they did exist, she was convinced they came from a different dimension, a different time. She didn't believe in heaven and hell and thus didn't believe a realm between the two existed for spirits to occupy, waiting to get into one or the other. The building was rich in history, so from her perspective, restless spirits of yesteryear might find the inn attractive and want to revisit as another form of energy—to relive the good ole days.

It was early evening before Molly could shake off the incident in Room 202. The first time it happened, it was weird; the second time, it was just downright bizarre. Truth be told, she was a little rattled. She wished she were more like Kai—more grounded. Kai saw the world in black and white; Molly lived in a world with multiple gradients of gray. She saw complexity and nuance in everything and everybody. It drove her ex-husband crazy—not that she cared what he thought.

Molly went about her usual business, preparing a light spread of hors d'oeuvres for the guests to enjoy when they returned from the beach. She made a charcuterie plate with meats and cheeses from local farms and fresh guacamole made with avocados and local heirloom tomatoes, uncorking a couple of red and rosé wines to go along with the food.

After cleaning up the kitchen, she returned to the owner's suite for the night. It was Kai's turn to take the helm. They alternated shifts throughout the day, each working two shifts. Molly had the morning and late-afternoon shifts, and Kai had the lunch and late-evening shifts.

It must have been the gin and tonic she gulped down that got her started on the computer. Molly ignored her inbox and searched the internet to see if there were other instances of wet towels in the paranormal world. She couldn't find anything similar, but she read about ectoplasm and wondered if the towels represented the exteriorizing of a spirit's communication.

"Wake up, Molly," Kai said, "you have to see this." Molly had drifted off during the Rachel Maddow Show. She roused herself, and seeing Kai's ashen face, realized her partner was panic-stricken.

"What is it?" Molly lifted herself up on her elbows, her old Tori Amos T-shirt hitching up under her breasts.

"Room 202," Kai said.

"Towels again?"

"No, something much weirder." She grabbed Molly by the wrist to lead her. Molly quickly got into her on-duty clothes and followed Kai up the stairs to the second floor. A few guests milled around outside their rooms while others gathered on the stairs. They watched her approach with questions on their faces.

Kai knocked and pushed through the door without waiting for an answer. Stanford was pacing back and forth at the base of the queen-sized bed. His eyes were red, either from crying, or fear, or both.

"What happened?" Molly asked. "Where's the professor?"

Stanford hesitated and looked at Kai for a cue how to respond.

"Tell her," Kai said, "you can trust her." He sniffled and ran the back of his hand under his tanned nose.

"He's gone." His voice cracked.

"What do you mean he's gone?" Molly asked. A sense of dread percolated inside her.

"We were in bed. I went to the bathroom, and when I returned, he was gone. He disappeared right in front of my eyes." Stanford sat down on a bench at the foot of the bed and lowered his head into his hands.

Molly looked around. "Maybe he just left."

"Why would he do that?" His voice pitched up several octaves.

"I don't know."

"It doesn't make sense," Stanford continued, "plus, look, nothing's missing. His wallet and keys are here, his suitcase and clothes over there, and his computer is still on the desk. The professor never went anywhere without that thing."

"Tell her what you noticed when you returned from the bathroom," Kai said. She moved over and placed her hand on his back to console him.

Stanford sniffled again and sat upright. "The bed was wet. Not watery wet like the towels, but gooey wet."

"Are you sure?" Molly inched closer to the bed and patted the handmade comforter. "The bed's dry."

"Yes, I'm sure." He turned his hands upward toward Kai and rolled his eyes. "Plus, there was a strange smell, like a burning smell. It wasn't nasty like rotten eggs, but sweet like molasses."

Molly thought of the article she read about ectoplasm and acted on impulse.

"What are you doing?" Kai yelled. She tried to grab Molly's wrist, but was too late. Stanford jumped to his feet and turned toward the bed. They both watched Molly jump onto the middle section of the bed on her back with her feet and arms spread out. She moved her arms and legs back and forth, like she was making a snow angel.

"See," Molly said, "nothing's happening." But then, something did happen. A loud groan—not quite a growl, more like a belch—shook the prisms on the chandelier overhead. The windows rattled like a Category 5 hurricane was raging outside. Kai dashed over to the side of the bed. It was too late.

A crater formed in the middle of the bed, revealing a cavernous hollow underneath with no bottom. Molly lay suspended above the crater, buoyed in midair by a bluish-green gelatinous liquid. Lightning bolts of yellow energy like veins pulsated through the fluid. A sweet burning smell, as Stanford described, filled the air.

A storm of fear invaded Molly's face. She tried to move, but her body didn't respond. She opened her mouth to scream, but no sound came out. In a flash, she was sucked down into a vortex. From below, she saw Room 202 disappear.

Kai's and Stanford's faces turned aghast, their mouths hanging open. They watched the bed surface reform over the crater, looked at each other, and then back at the bed. There were no words to describe what they had just witnessed.

Below, Molly floated through the gelatin-like fluid. She could breathe—she inhaled and exhaled to make sure. Moving her arms and legs around through the liquid and shifting her body, she realized she had no sense of up or down. It felt like swimming, but took no effort, as if there was no gravity. The sharpened edge of fear dulled into curiosity.

The sea surrounded her. Schools of fish in all sizes and colors swam by. Crabs, shrimp, clams, and mussels swirled in the murky water. She was in the ocean, but she wasn't.

She found herself in some sort of pod, surrounded by projections of scenes as if she were watching a movie. She tried to make sense of the images, which seemed to be views from high above the water. Dark, intense storms thrashed the coastline. Huge walls of water caused buildings to crash into the sea. Hundreds of thousands of dead bodies floated in the wake. Whole beaches disappeared. Entire communities vanished. Miles and miles of land were overtaken by water.

A sense of gloom gripped her as Molly tried to figure out what was going on. She thrashed her arms and legs, but to no avail. The liquid encasing her turned colder. Goosebumps formed on her skin. A glimmer of light allowed her to see Dr. Hobson, who had appeared next to her. His face was puffy, and bags had formed under his eyes. "Can you hear me?" Molly asked. Dr. Hobson nodded. She felt something on the left side of her head. It was a strange feeling and tingled, as if her brain were being massaged. Her left eye twitched, and then she saw a white flash. Strange, whispering sounds echoed in her head. She placed her hands over her ears. The sounds continued for a short time, then stopped. She shook her head. Realizing there was now ground below, she struggled to her feet and stood, a bit wobbly, beside the professor.

"Are you OK?" he asked.

Molly nodded as she rubbed her eyes. "Where are we?"

"It's not *where* are we," Dr. Hobson replied, "it's *when* are we."

"What does that mean?"

"I'm pretty sure we travelled through time based on the wormhole projections. We're in a different time, perhaps a different dimension. I think we're in the future."

"Why are we here?"

Dr. Hobson didn't answer. The world around them looked dead, dark, and desolate. There were no signs of life. Then a spark flared in Molly's head. Her eyeballs flickered back in her eye sockets. She raised her hands up with her palms facing out and stretched open. Her body shook with violent ferocity, then stopped. Her muscles relaxed and her head tilted forward.

"Molly," Dr. Hobson said, "Molly, are you all right?"

Molly felt weak and tried to regain the strength to talk. She shook her head to get the cobwebs out. "I'm OK, I think." Her voice caught. She could hear other voices.

"What happened to you?" Dr. Hobson asked. "You were convulsing like you were possessed."

"They want to know if you're going to change," Molly said. "I can hear them."

"Who's 'they' and change what?"

"Change the way you think. They, the guardians, the forces that represent nature—they're the ones who brought you here. They say you've become deaf to the truth and are ignoring what is obvious. They brought me here to communicate with you. They want to know if you're going to continue in denial."

The professor looked stunned.

"Well?"

"I don't think I can," he whispered.

"They told me that if you don't listen, they will have to find other ways to communicate with you. And that those methods might be . . . drastic."

A loud, deep sound jarred them and rattled their teeth. Molly felt a sensation in her stomach like she was freefalling. The projected images appeared to be going in reverse, but much faster this time.

She saw light in front of her as Room 202 appeared. In a flash, she was on the bed, gasping for breath. Kai and Stanford jumped up and approached her. Molly sat up, scraping remnants of the gelatinous fluid off her arms.

"We have to get out," Molly yelled. Her eyes were wide with fear. The room shook as though a magnitude 8.0 earthquake had struck.

"What?" Kai asked.

"They said they would send a sign to warn the professor. This must be what they meant."

"Who's 'they?' "

"The forces," Molly said. "Round up the guests and get out." The crystal chandelier shattered and fell to the bed. They ran from Room 202 and shouted for the guests to leave. They fled out the front door as water smashed through every window and blew off the roof. A torrent of water shot upwards.

"What's going on?" Kai yelled. The inn caved in just as the last guests escaped.

"A warning," Molly said. She wrapped her arm around Kai and pulled her close.

Doctor Hobson appeared at their side. He was covered in the same gelatinous goo as Molly. A musky, burning odor filled the air. His hand shook as he rubbed his eyes. Fear was etched across his face. His lips moved.

"Say that again," Molly said, as she and Kai turned towards the professor. He cleared his throat.

"And the sea hath spoken."

DARRYL FORREST WAS BORN IN DENVER, CO AND HAS AN ENGLISH DEGREE FROM THE UNIVERSITY OF MARYLAND BALTIMORE COUNTY. HE'S LIVED IN FAIRFAX, VA, FOR OVER TWENTY YEARS WITH HIS WIFE—SHORT STORY WRITER AND ARTIST, EMILY ZASADA—AND THEIR SON. DARRYL HAS AN AVID INTEREST IN STORIES ABOUT CLIMATE CHANGE AND IS CONCERNED ABOUT THE CHANGES HE HAS SEEN IN THE MID-ATLANTIC CLIMATE DURING HIS LIFETIME. HE IS ALSO INTERESTED IN THE USE OF TECHNOLOGY TO INFLUENCE THOUGHT, WINE, DRONES, JAZZ, AND THE CULTURE AROUND THE SEARCH FOR BIGFOOT. HE WRITES FICTION FOR FUN.

Lefty and the Empty Bucket of Fries

By Tony Houck

The seaweed resembled wilted lettuce, and a decaying head of it had been left on the beach in darkness by high tide. A ghost crab had scavenged the cluster of green "leaves" and then abandoned it at dawn, darting back to its burrow to escape a fisherman spiking his rod holders into the sand. By early afternoon, the sea lettuce's fishiness and sliminess had been baked out of it by the August sun.

Now brown and crispy, the seaweed still lay on the beach. A woman stood near it, as the pounding surf drowned out her flat stomach's growls for dinner. She slipped the crochet lace tote off her shoulder and opened it: sunscreen, sunglasses, next-generation e-reader, this year's best smartphone, two half-drunk bottles of designer water, protein bar, calfskin leather clutch. She palmed her phone, closed and re-shouldered her tote, and tried to resume ignoring her young daughter, but couldn't. "Don't touch that," she told the girl, disgusted by the seaweed. "Don't even poke at it with your toes. You'll ruin your nail polish. Come here."

After rolling her eyes, the eight-year-old stomped back to her mother, staying just out of her reach, and went back to pouting. Bow-tie pigtails, sunflower dress, strappy sandals, ladylike purse—Zara was the epitome of summer style as she stood there, arms crossed, lower lip thrust out into the muggy late afternoon.

The tide was rising again and sent waves rushing up the beach. The water thinned into a bubbly film that wetted the dry sand near Zara and her mother. The swash retreated to the sea.

Zara's mother backpedaled and lifted her pedicured feet in turn and twisted them around, inspecting her sandals. Although the rhinestone slides were dry, she turned to her daughter and said, "Time to go."

"To the boardwalk? Back to Ryan's?"

"No," Zara's mother said flatly, extending her hand. "Come, it's time for dinner."

The eight-year-old's arms stayed crossed, but she relaxed her lip. "I'm not eating unless we go back to Ryan's."

Puckering her nose, Zara's mother shook her head. "I'm not taking you back to Ryan's, and we're not getting one of those *things*. Don't ask me again." She turned on her smartphone. *I missed the wine society meetup for this?* she asked herself, scrolling through the phone's missed calls log. She recognized both numbers: gal pals and fellow American Wine Society members who also belonged to the Rehoboth Beach Country Club. *Probably wanted to rant and rave about those blended cabernets from Napa at lunch. Or talk about the catering for the club's fall golf tournament.* The gals hadn't left a message, but she would call them back anyway, after Zara went to bed—if she ever went to bed. Zara's intolerably late summer vacation bedtime was her father's doing. *School can't start soon enough.* She dialed her husband's number.

"Who are you calling?" Zara asked her.

"Daddy."

"What for?"

The woman pressed SEND, lifted the brim of her floppy hat, and put the phone to her ear. "To tell him that I've changed my mind about meeting at the Blue Moon for dinner. That we're getting in the car and going home."

"What will you have for dinner, then?" Zara asked her. *"I'm* still not eating until I go to Ryan's."

"Lori's Cafe delivers. Or Daddy can pick up something on his way home." She listened to the phone ring until her husband, a Delaware family law attorney, answered. "Are you still at the courthouse?" she asked him curtly, cutting him off in mid-hello and then listening to his answer. "You're here at Dolles?"

Zara stuck out her tongue at her mother and lilted up the beach toward Dolles and her father, who had paused under the big sign to take his wife's call.

The woman gave her husband a halfhearted wave and spoke again into the phone: "It's your turn to deal with her . . . I don't care what you do or where you eat . . . I have food with me . . . I'm going to sit on a bench and read. Or count the days until school starts. I might just go home."

She told her husband goodbye and hung up without asking him if he had won or lost his client's divorce case.

Moments later, Zara marched down the boardwalk with her father in tow. She had had him wrapped around her finger since she was a baby, and undeterred by her mother's nose puckering, Zara was going to get what she wanted.

She towed her father up to Ryan's and stopped in front of a blue-painted cart. Its lone, red wheel was just for show. Above it, on one of several yellow-and-orange shelves, was a large cage with paper signs tied to it. Hermit crabs with nearly identical, natural shells slumbered or clunked around in the bottom of the cage. Bare-bones, clear plastic "crabitats" of various sizes filled the shelves. Wire containers labeled "My Hermit Crab Condo" hung from the cart's top and sides. Painted shells—selling for $1.59 each or $3.00 for two—filled a plastic tub screwed to the front of the cart.

"That hermit crab right there, Daddy," Zara told him sugar-sweetly, pointing inside the cage.

"Which one?" her father asked. "They all look the same."

"No, they don't. The one on the coral is the biggest."

Zara's father glanced around the cage and watched a crab in a shell slightly larger than the other ones climb a colony of coral. "You're right. He is bigger than all the others." The man took a deep breath. "What did Mommy say about all this?"

Zara let go of her father's hand. "She said to make sure to buy everything we need to take care of it. And to make sure to get the one I want."

"Are you sure that's what Mommy—"

"And I want that one. And his name will be Shelly," Zara said. "And he will be free," she continued, pointing at a paper sign, "because we're purchasing a cage." She slid her purse up to her elbow and with two hands grabbed a crabitat with a bright-green lid. Inside it were the barest essentials of hermit crab life: a thin layer of rainbow gravel and a bleached clam shell. Zara handed the crabitat to her father and seized a chartreuse shell with black polka dots from the tub of painted shells. "I saw this one when I was here with Mommy," Zara said. "Don't you like how it and the lid of the crabitat are the same color?"

"I certainly do, but I'm not sure about—"

"Shelly's going to get even bigger. And when he does, he's going to move into this green shell. He needs food and other things, too. We'll get them after." Zara pointed at another paper sign. "Go ask for assistance, Daddy. You aren't allowed to open the cage."

Zara's father checked the lid of the crabitat and grabbed it by the handle. With his free hand, he reached into his pocket. "Maybe we should call Mommy first," he said, pulling out his phone—last year's best smartphone.

Zara grabbed him by the belt loop. "We have to ask for assistance,

Daddy. And we need to buy supplies for Shelly." She towed her father inside the store.

*****

The beach chair was an "I'm sorry I bought our daughter a hermit crab" gift. It had a thick pillow headrest, cushioned arms, and a low-profile design, but as Zara's mother sat sulking on the beach, its best feature was a drink holder. She lifted her floppy hat to uncover an open pinot noir spritzer, took another *light and fruity*-flavored sip from the bottle, and returned the drink to the holder. Alcoholic beverages were prohibited on Rehoboth Beach, but her slight spritzer buzz would have been worth any reprimand or citation.

She opened the tote resting on her lap and pulled out her e-reader. Unlike her old one, this next-generation device had a built-in light that allowed decent reading in sunlight. Zara had given her only two minutes' peace all afternoon, but now, at twilight, Zara's mother was finally alone. Well, almost alone. She opened the leather case, waking up the device. Page three of this week's bestselling novel popped off the screen in high definition. She started to read.

High tide had retreated to a quieter sea, and she could hear Shelly clunking around in his now furnished crabitat. Zara had left it next to her when she left to tow her father to Funland. With a disgusted sigh, Zara's mother slammed the e-reader closed and glared over the arm of the chair at Shelly. If, like a magician, she could have made that little crab and its home disappear by covering them with her hat, she would have. Instead, she dug the back of her head into the chair's thick pillow, gulped down her spritzer, set the empty bottle in the drink holder, and dropped her hat over it.

She adjusted the chair. And then again. And again. None of the four sitting positions were *incredibly comfortable,* despite what the tag had read. She settled on slightly reclined.

A moment later, she sat up and twisted herself around to look at the boardwalk. The lights were on. She couldn't see Zara, her husband, or the giant stuffed dog or lobster or walrus that Zara would have cajoled him into winning for her at the expense of God knows how many quarters. She glanced up the beach, and then down it. She twisted herself back around, leaned back, and quickly sat up again. There was no sign of them in any direction.

She fully reclined the chair and settled back into the headrest. Her spritzer buzz-assisted hand reached under the arm of the chair, popped the top off the crabitat, and pushed it onto the beach. Her hand returned to the e-reader. She opened it and pretended to read the bestseller, keeping an ear on Shelly.

She didn't have to wait long—the crunch of rainbow gravel, scratching sounds on driftwood and then on plastic, a thump on the sand.

She rolled her head to the side and watched the hermit crab emerge from its shell and walk away. Tiny, red claws, legs, and antennae heading up the beach and out of her life.

She put the lid back on the crabitat but did not snap it shut. *Make sure you act surprised when Zara finds him missing and then blame her for not putting the lid on tightly,* she told herself, rolling her head back and returning her hand and eyes to the e-reader. The text was crisp and bright, but she didn't read a word of it. "If he thinks Zara's getting another hermit crab," she mumbled to herself, now hoping for her family to return, "he's going to need an attorney to represent *him* in a divorce."

* * * * *

Although the name "hermit crab" belied Shelly's gregarious nature, the little escape artist (actually, he was more of an opportunist) had survived the night by himself.

A scavenger by nature, he had found ample food on the dunes, including crunchy leaves, discarded apple cores and banana peels, and littered dregs of popcorn. As the first fingers of dawn caressed the shore, he dragged the hard end of a Thrasher's French fry toward the dune where Zara had made a spectacle of herself upon finding her new pet missing. With less drama and more looking, she might have found him.

Dragging his food for the day, Shelly approached the burrow he had dug for himself. Hidden among new shoots of beach grass, the entrance to the long and narrow hole had collapsed. He tunneled his way inside, pinched off a clawful of fry, and fed on the vinegary bit. A dab of ketchup would have been a treat, but on Thrasher's fries, *that* condiment provoked scowls and derision. Shelly's instinctive brain didn't meditate on the quirks of humans, but he appreciated their propensity for gluttony. He retracted into his shell and slept.

The August sun beat down on Shelly's sandy hollow throughout the day. He stirred occasionally to feed. Nocturnal by nature, he emerged from his shell as the new moon rose. He finished the French fry and tunneled deeper into the dune. In the middle of the night, he poked his antennae outside, sensing for shore birds that could peck him to death, and then left his burrow. The new shoots of beach grass twitched as he crawled through them, toward the boardwalk. Protected by the darkness of the new moon and a broken pole light, he reveled in the moist sand around a foot washing station and scavenged around a trash can. He returned to his burrow to eat and sleep. The rising sun tucked him in.

Shelly's day repeated itself. And then again. Again and again, until it was time for him to molt. But there wasn't a chartreuse-painted shell with black polka dots for him to move his larger self into.

On a warm night in an otherwise cool October, as a hurricane churned hundreds of miles offshore, Shelly ventured away from his burrow, heading toward the wide strand of debris left by the receding high tide. Sensing real and imagined dangers, he continually retracted into and emerged from his undersized shell as he walked along the beach.

His gregariousness drew him toward a ghost crab. Not as social as Shelly, it hurried away toward a large clump of seaweed. Unaware that the little ghost often preyed on other crabs, Shelly followed it. With plentiful debris to scavenge and in no competition for shells—since ghost crabs conceal themselves in burrows, not shells—the pair coexisted. Shelly eventually moved on.

After an hour-long search, he found a sea snail's spirally coiled shell. It was empty and intact and suitable for a hermit crab's long, curved, soft body. Shelly stood beside the new shell, flicking his antennae back and forth as he sensed for danger. He unclasped his abdomen, left his undersized shell, and tried on the new one. It was also too small for him to retract fully inside it, and he quickly returned to his old shell and continued searching.

At four in the morning, an hour before the beach would open and in violation of the leash law, a beachcomber's Labrador puppy spotted Shelly and bounded toward him on feet that were still too big for it. Shelly retracted as far as he could into his shell and incompletely sealed himself inside it with his large, left claw. The puppy sniffed him, rolled him around with its nose, and mouthed him like a tennis ball. Then, carrying its new toy and with its tail wagging proudly, the puppy returned to its master.

Shelly defended himself.

The Lab yelped in pain, shook the pinching critter out of its mouth, and hid between its master's legs. After thudding on the sand, Shelly lay there in his shell, playing dead but irrevocably disabled.

The beachcomber unfolded the leash he was carrying and restrained the puppy. He checked its paws and then pried open its mouth and explored it with his fingers. He found something hard stuck in the puppy's gums. The Lab yelped again as the beachcomber gently removed the object.

The beachcomber petted the puppy reassuringly and inspected what he had found. Lying in his palm, and barely visible in the pre-dawn light, was the severed claw of a hermit crab. Having owned several of the little critters when he was young, the beachcomber knew it was the larger, left claw, which the crab used to defend itself and seal itself into its shell (it used its right claw to feed and scoop water up to its mouth). The beachcomber wrinkled his forehead, a frown of confusion. He had seen land hermit crabs around the lower Chesapeake Bay but never on Rehoboth Beach. *It must have escaped from one of those cages on the boardwalk,* he thought to himself, walking to where the puppy had dropped its toy. The Lab followed him.

As a hungry, keen-eyed sandpiper took in the scene, the beachcomber picked up Shelly. He showed him to the puppy, which backed away from him. He turned the hermit crab over. The sight saddened him. "Well, he *is* a throwaway pet. And he'll never survive on his own now," he told the suddenly shell-skittish puppy.

With those words, Shelly's beach life came to an end. The beachcomber headed for the boardwalk and a trash can.

* * * * *

The January sun streaked through the clouds and brightened the beachcomber's study. On the carpeted floor, the Labrador puppy, now grown into its feet, lay stretched across a pillow bed. The sound of kibble plunking into a metal bowl roused him. He rose and stretched, leaning backward and then forward. Now more curious than afraid of little critters that lived in shells, he sniffed a freestanding glass aquarium, leaving nose prints on it. Burrowed into a thick layer of moist sand warmed by an under-tank heater, Shelly continued to sleep away the day. He had all night to play on his climbing net and coconut castle, to munch on bananas and carrots, and to scoop fresh water and saltwater out of his two ceramic bowls. The puppy ran to the kitchen.

As the Lab chowed down on kibble, its bowl clanged against a wooden recycling bin. Into that bin, three months ago, the beachcomber had dropped an empty, grease-stained bucket of Thrasher's French fries. He had gotten it out of a trash can on the boardwalk, banged the dregs out of it, and carried Shelly home in it. And by the time he had walked into his study with the disabled critter, he had given his new pet a name—Lefty.

If Shelly had known about his pampered future, he might not have been so scared in that Thrasher's bucket. He would have poked more than his antennae out of his shell and explored. He might even have made his way all the way around the inside of the bucket. But he wouldn't have found so much as a drop of ketchup.

Tony Houck is a former information specialist and technical Spanish translator who now writes full-time. His first novel, *The Precariousness of Done*, which is set in the Spanish town where he lived and studied, is scheduled for public release in early 2018. He is currently working on two other novels and is owner and operator of the blog *Unsalted Gems* (https://tonyhouck.com), which focuses on travel, Spanish language and culture, crazy families, writing and getting published, and obsessive-compulsive disorder, from which he has suffered for most of his life. He resides in Fredericksburg, Virginia, with his wife, son, and their pound puppy, all of whom are bitten by the bug to travel and explore.

"Lefty and the Empty Bucket of Fries" is one of those stories that opens with a situation, blossoms into a worrisome event, and ends with a happy ending. One would not think that a story about a crab could grab one's interest, but this is a good, fun beach read. Kudos to Tony Houck.

Bottleneck at Hole 14

By Renay Regardie

Saturday morning. Dismal. Gray. Chilly. None of the things you want on a June weekend at the beach. Certainly none of the things you want when your son, daughter-in-law, and their three kids are here for the weekend. Three kids, ages fourteen, twelve, and six, confined to your house. Watch that house shrink as raindrops pelt the windows.

No, no, make the rain go away, I prayed to any god who might hear me. Anyone—sun god, rain god, weather god—*please.*

My praying got through, at least enough so that the rain stopped. The wind still blew, the sky remained leaden, the temperature moved up to a passable seventy-one degrees. I breathed in the damp air gratefully. It won't be a total bust, I told myself.

We prepare to schlep to the beach. The Red Flyer is ready to load. We drag out the favored beach toys: the big bucket, the blue shovel (the six-year-old's favorite), the red one, too, the starfish sand toy, one big ball, one small water skimmer, three boogie boards, one skimboard. Throw in a few snacks: red grapes, goldfish, watermelon slices, six bottles of water. We're ready to go.

We haul everything across the street to the beach. The boys are in the lead, pulling the wagon overburdened with toys, towels, snacks, and a forty-five-pound granddaughter. My husband and I trudge along at the rear.

I'd envisioned a day that would be easy. Early on, the kids would frolic at the beach, their parents overseeing. Later that afternoon, my husband and I would take them to miniature golf, followed by pizza, while the parents partied with friends. The kids knew if everything went well (that means they behaved themselves reasonably), there'd be an extra sweet treat in it for them.

The better the day, the better the moods of the kids and their grandparents while they hunker down to an hour-and-a-half of mini-golf, followed by a boisterous dinner. Nevertheless, I was on edge.

Not that I don't like being with my grandkids. I do. In measured doses.

I used to love the beach. Now I love pictures of the beach. Three years ago, we built a backyard pool. I love controlled pool temperature at eighty-five degrees. I love waveless water no more than five feet deep. I love dangling my feet at the edge of the pool. I love pretending I'm mad when my granddaughter sprays me with her water pistol.

I don't love stiff winds at the beach. I don't love sand in my hair. I don't love wrapping myself in two towels because I'm cold. I don't love fierce and frigid waves trying to knock me over.

Despite this, there are things I love today about this beach. The waves are wild, and the red boundary flag flaps crazily. The rising tide has created large pools of water, only inches deep. I move close and dip my toe in, expecting an icy chill assaulting my leg. But the water is not cold at all, despite the chilly air, despite the sign that says the ocean temperature is sixty-six degrees. This water is placid. I can wade in this.

Max, the fourteen-year-old, practices on his skimboard. He's improved markedly since last year. Sam paddles around sideways across three boogie boards. Rachel happily splashes herself and anyone within three feet.

I sit back, thinking I might dive into *A Gentleman in Moscow* on my Kindle, when the sky suddenly darkens and raindrops dot my new bathing suit.

We jump up. We run.

We make it home before the sky opens up, before the rain roars through, soaking the porch furniture, before the wind whips our Washington Nationals flag out of its holder, pushing our team's emblem into the sodden earth.

Then a summer god miracle. As quickly as it erupted, the rain and wind subside, the sun blasts through. Warm air caresses my skin.

Mini-golf will proceed. Two grandparents will not be stuck in the house with three high-energy grandkids.

Mini-golf has become a grandparent/grandkid beach ritual. I can't say it's exactly a bonding experience, because the game is too often fraught with shouts of "He cheated" and "It's my turn to be first," or sobs of "He's being so mean to me," followed by a cry of "Just hit the damn ball," uttered from my husband's lips (not mine, I'm sure).

Despite the decades I have on these kids, I still like to win. Everyone should have a good time, but I'm going to play my hardest.

When we arrive at Shell We Golf on Route One—my favorite mini-golf course in the Rehoboth area—we survey the parking lot. Today, only a few cars, a good sign since I don't tolerate lines well.

We walk up to the ticket booth, and I fork over $40 for the five of us. We spend time picking out our ball color. Max grabs orange, Sam considers carefully and settles on yellow, Rachel goes for light blue, her favorite color. I always want the lavender ball—it matches my nail polish. My husband, in a darkish mood, picks navy.

We always talk about practicing, but when we arrive, we are so excited, we rush up to the first tee.

Our scorekeeper today is fourteen-year-old Max. Sometimes, it's my husband, but we decided last year that he took too long toting up the results, plus his addition was spotty.

Our six-year-old announces her score will not be counted today. I am relieved. I don't need jeers from her brothers and tears from her. Today we are in luck. Due to the earlier rain, there is no line at Hole 1. Rachel goes first. The first hole is a straight shot. Rachel hits a great ball that bounces along the far wall and comes to rest three feet from the cup. She gloats. Sam hits a line drive that bounces over the hole. Max's shot is a bit too strong. I'm up next. I grasp my club, eye the target, bend into my pretend golf stance, swing, and the ball goes into the cup. I have hit a hole in one. I hoot wildly. Everyone looks at me in disbelief.

The second hole is more challenging. There's a curve, and you hope to bounce your ball along the wall so that it careens around, avoiding the rock hazard. I'm up first. I hope only to avoid the rocks. I bend over, swing through, and—gasp—another hole in one! I am giddy. No one is as happy with me as I am with me.

My giddiness doesn't last long. I get a six on the next hole, the maximum allowed. Our scorekeeper smiles. He's steady at twos and threes.

The game proceeds. At Hole 6, Rachel begs to go first. Our scorekeeper says it's not her turn. Her mouth turns down. I exert Grandmother Authority, and she hits a line drive that pops over to the next hole. We applaud her strength.

We come to Hole 8, where I hit another hole in one. I am back in the game. I am not the crowd favorite.

At the end of nine holes, I'm behind Max by three strokes, and Sam is right on my tail.

My husband has faded badly, probably due to the fact that he has tried to show how well he can putt with one hand. His non-skill at backward shots has not helped his score, either.

Heading into the back nine, it's anyone's game.

Things are tougher on that back nine. More slope, more water, more frayed tempers.

We come to Hole 12, my favorite. There's a roaring stream (well, a mildly bubbling brook) to the right. Straight ahead, there's a cup that will spit your ball right out at the hole. Your instinct is to try to hole it. Don't. Go for the water. The current will whisk your ball back and forth, then grab it, pushing it through a tunnel, where it lands a foot from the hole. We all do this. Our balls kiss each other. We all make twos.

We've been playing for over an hour. Puffy clouds dance above us. A gentle breeze blows. What a day! Playing mini-golf with your grandkids can be so rewarding. There have been no meltdowns, no fistfights, no clamors of a need for the bathroom, no whining for ice cream. Only six holes to go. I can almost taste that ice-cold glass of sauvignon blanc that awaits me—my reward for grandma duty well done.

As we tee up for Hole 13, I note that the course has become busier. No one's on our tail, eyeing us nastily because we're a party of five instead of the regulation four. Still, there's no longer time to dawdle, no longer time for little victory dances.

Hole 13 is a straight shot to a mildly elevated tee, one of the easier holes on the course. So easy, in fact, that the kids have already finished as my husband and I are lining up our shots.

The kids are waiting on Hole 14, which is raised several feet above Hole 13. I hear them hooting and laughing. This hole is a challenge. You approach the hole through a wide stone arch, with water cascading around. To me, it's a little Magic Kingdom kitsch.

"Stop horsing around," I yell up to them, having no idea what's going on. I hope the boys are not teasing Rachel, that we don't have a meltdown.

I walk through the Magic Kingdom arches to find all three staring at me.

"My ball is stuck," says Rachel.

"Uh, we had a little accident," says Max.

Let me explain the dynamics of Hole 14. The approach is elevated around five feet above the target. If, by luck, you hit straight ahead, your ball will drop into the top hole, travel down through a curved tunnel, and emerge below, inches from your target. The safety play is to hit to the left, banking your ball around a curve.

Today there is a problem.

Max has grabbed Sam's near-empty water bottle and tossed it in the air. "I meant to catch it," he says, "but I missed and it fell into the hole."

"My ball is stuck," wails Rachel.

I don't believe it. I look into the top hole. I see no plastic bottle stuck in there. I shove in my club. It dislodges nothing. I think they are joshing me.

I tee up my lavender ball. I hit it straight ahead—straight for that little hole—and it rolls in. Wow, another hole in one!

But the ball does not come out the spout below. The lavender ball must be lodged behind the light-blue ball, which must be pressing against a near-empty plastic Aquafina water bottle stuck in the tunnel where it curves before it straightens to spit out a golf ball. The tunnel is not designed to spit out a water bottle.

"We have to tell. Come on, Max." I grab Max in an ungrandmotherly way. I stride toward the ticket taker's booth. Max slumps behind.

The old guy seems nonplussed. I have to repeat my story until he gets it. Yeah, there's a problem on Hole 14, and now that the course is busier, there's a potential bottleneck building. Slowly, he leaves the safety of his booth and treks over to Hole 14. We follow.

By now, someone else is playing Hole 14, despite the fact that my husband and Sam are still standing there. The ticket guy peers into the hole and sticks a golf club in, just as I did. He moves down to the spout, peers in, sticks a club in. Nothing.

"I'll try to hose it out," he says. "Hey, just get another ball."

"Hurry up," I say to my group. People are waiting. I see two parties behind us with hands on hips, often the precursor to get-moving shouts.

We agree to give everyone a three on Hole 14.

Our misadventure on that hole has turned a blue sky into one streaked with gray. We play Hole 15 quickly and silently, attempting to distance ourselves from the parties tied up behind us. My pulse returns to normal as I hear no cries of "My ball's stuck in the tunnel."

The brothers tussle on Hole 16. Hole 17—the hardest one on the course—brings tears to Rachel's eyes as one brother shouts at her to hurry up. I hug her. I promise her candy. The tears stop.

Thankfully, the last hole is uneventful.

We all try to win a free game on the pretend nineteenth hole, which is the course's ball retriever. We swing. No one hits into the winning slot. This has not been our lucky day.

Everything feels anticlimactic, including the fact that our scorekeeper is the winner. Still, that doesn't prevent Max from reminding his grandfather that he promised the winner five bucks. Grandpa forks the bill over.

As we return our clubs, I ask the ticket taker, "Did you get the ball out?"

"Nope," he says, "not yet."

But our game is done, and we've got a great story to tell and a dinner to eat. We head toward the Shell We Golf parking lot.

EPILOGUE

In the days following the disappearance of two balls at Hole 14 at the Shell We Golf mini-golf course in Rehoboth Beach, Delaware, I had visions of stunned players peering into the top crevice, sticking their club in, then examining the exit spout. I pictured backed-up colored golf balls spewing out of the top cup. I imagined snarls from grown men, frustration from moms, tears from seven-year-olds. I saw angry people yelling at the ticket taker, asking for their money back—or at least their money back for Hole 14. I dreamed I saw a sign, "Hole 14 Closed. Under Repair."

I felt it necessary to return to the scene of the crime, uh, event. I went on a Monday, early in the morning, figuring there would be fewer witnesses. The sky was cloudless, the parking lot, full. I selected the lavender ball and took a scorecard to keep up appearances. I tried to make a beeline for Hole 14, but the course was busy. I nimbly elbowed my way around parents and their broods. I almost clipped one kid with my club, and picked up my pace as his father glared at me.

A mom and her five-year-old were dawdling around Hole 14. When she saw me approaching with my club out at sword height, she hurried him along, ignoring his cries for a do-over.

I carefully teed up my ball, got into my stance, swung, and watched the ball roll into the top hole. The ball came out of the spout, clipped the target hole, and rested quietly two feet away. The tunnel was unplugged! Mini-golf was saved.

The grandkids will be back in two weeks. We'll have another mini-golf tournament.

This time, no water bottles allowed.

RENAY REGARDIE BUILT, AND THEN SOLD, A BUSINESS THAT PROVIDED MARKET RESEARCH, FEASIBILITY STUDIES, AND MARKETING STRATEGY TO RESIDENTIAL HOME DEVELOPERS. ARMED WITH YEARS OF BUSINESS WRITING, SHE TURNED BACK TO HER FIRST LOVE, WRITING. SHE ESPECIALLY GIVES THANKS TO THE GUIDANCE AND SUPPORT OF MARIBETH FISCHER AND EVERYONE CONNECTED WITH THE REHOBOTH BEACH WRITERS' GUILD. RENAY HAS HAD STORIES PUBLISHED IN THREE OF THE FOUR PREVIOUS REHOBOTH BEACH READS BOOKS. EACH SUMMER, RENAY'S FAMILY, INCLUDING FIVE GRANDCHILDREN, MEET UP AT THE BEACH FOR SUN AND FUN. SOMETIMES, STRANGE THINGS HAPPEN AT THE FAMILY'S MINI-GOLF ROUNDS. RENAY SPLITS HER TIME AMONG REHOBOTH, WASHINGTON, DC, AND KEY WEST.

The Shot Shared Round the World

By Joy Givens

Only another hour until the beach. It was the first day of summer vacation after junior year, but I'd spent most of it in the car. One more hour of ancient music with Mom, Dad, and occasionally Grandpa singing along. If we didn't get to the hotel before the playlist circled back to "Walk Like an Egyptian," I might have to climb out the sunroof.

Dad caught my eye in the rearview mirror from the driver's seat. "You okay, Leigh? Not getting carsick with that phone in your face, are you?"

I grimaced and nodded. "Fine, Dad." My phone vibrated.

"Omg Leigh." It was a text from Jenna.

"What?" I texted back.

Beside me, Mom sighed. "Are you sure you don't want to learn to crochet before we get there?"

I looked at the pile of colorful squares on her lap and the small mountain of yarn next to her. "No, thanks. I think that actually *would* make me carsick."

"You just spend so much time on that phone. This is family week. Aren't you excited to see the cousins? You could all help finish Aunt Sophia's blanket together. Chelsea and Karlie said they can't wait to learn. They even texted me about it!"

She sounded proud. Oh, Mom and her flip phone. She had resisted upgrades longer than anyone I knew, calling herself a "digital dinosaur."

My phone vibrated again. In the passenger seat, Grandpa gasped and started coughing.

"You okay, Dad?" Mom dropped her hook and laid a hand on his shoulder.

"Fine, fi-fine," he blustered. "Swallowed some air, is all."

"You don't feel dizzy, or faint, or—"

"I'm fine," he insisted. "Don't worry about me. Worry about all the ladies I'll be charming on the Rehoboth boardwalk this week."

Mom rolled her eyes. "Dad—"

Grandpa coughed again and cleared his throat. "What? You don't think all this is going to just sit on the shelf this week, do you?" He clenched his cellphone and flexed an old-man bicep through the sleeve of his Hawaiian shirt.

I smirked and looked back at my phone. Grandpa would keep them busy. Then I could—

Wait.

What had Jenna just texted me? Oh, no. I scrolled frantically, keeping my phone low enough that only I could see it.

Oh, *no*.

It was a screenshot of an Instagram photo from the Britt Allen concert two nights ago. The Britt Allen concert I wasn't allowed to attend because of finals but sneaked out to anyway by spending a "study night" at Jenna's. Jenna's cousin was friends with one of the roadies, and he had gotten us backstage. In the most epic moment of my life, we had met Britt herself and snapped photos with her.

And now, the most ridiculous face I'd ever made in a photo had hit social media.

In my photo, my face was split into what could only be called a deranged grin. With my red hair loose down my back, I looked like a rabid hyena, stupid-giggling over Britt Allen, who was posing next to me.

And judging by the dozens of comments and thousands of likes, it had gone *viral*.

"Oh, sh . . ."

I trailed off as Mom looked up. *Don't make this situation worse.* "Sheesh, Grandpa," I managed. "You're not really going on any dates this week, are you?"

"Dates!" he scoffed. "No way, Peanut. What do the kids call it now . . . hooking up?"

"Dad!" Mom looked mortified.

Grandpa's shoulders shook with laughter, and I could see Dad chuckling to himself. I shrank into my seat, wishing I could deflate like a beach ball and hide in our trunk.

My phone started going crazy, like it was stuck on vibrate. Text after text after text:

"Leigh your famous!"

"Have u seen this tho?"

"U & Britt! Is this real?"

"What's w/ ur face?"

It was on Twitter, too. Someone had already captioned it: "Find someone who looks at you like this fan looks at Britt. #WhenTheBrittMeetsTheFan"

It had gotten nine thousand likes in under an hour. The hashtag was trending. I was officially a meme.

A text from Karlie vibrated onto my screen. "What's up girl? I thought you weren't allowed to go to that concert!"

"I wasn't," I texted back, adding three panic emojis and a row of death emojis.

Her reply was equally clear: "Nooooooooooooooooooooo! I'll tell Chels. We'll keep it quiet!"

Goosebumps rippled over my skin. Mom had a dinosaur phone and Dad was driving. But how long could I possibly keep this secret once we arrived? First day of summer and I was already dead.

"Girls, will you put those infernal things away?" My mom's sister Marilyn adjusted her wide-brimmed hat and stared at us.

"Sorry, Mom," Chelsea and Karlie said in unison, dropping their cellphones into our beach bag. We all popped up from the hotel beds and grabbed our towels.

"Sorry, Aunt Marilyn," I added.

"How did we ever survive without those things." She shook her head, but her eyes were amused. "Oh, yeah. We had *lives*. Now spray some SPF on each other so we can head down."

We had arrived around three o'clock and met up with my aunts, uncles, cousins, and Grandpa's sister Sophia. Dad, Grandpa, and Aunt Sophia were all taking it easy in their rooms, but the rest of us were going to get in an hour at the beach before dinner.

None of our parents (or Grandpa or Aunt Sophia, obviously) had said anything about my shot-shared-round-the-world, and the other cousins were all too young for Wi-Fi. Only Karlie and Chelsea—a year older and younger than me, respectively—knew about it.

Well, Karlie and Chelsea and fifty-thousand-plus strangers on the internet.

Aunt Marilyn slipped back into the hallway. "We're heading to the lobby, girls," she called over her shoulder. The door banged shut.

"We'll get some great spam shots on the beach," Chelsea said, spraying sunscreen on my shoulders.

Chelsea's idea was to "spam" up all our social media feeds with photos around Rehoboth. That, combined with deleting any tags or links to the viral photo from our own profiles, would hopefully minimize the chance that people who knew us would see it.

"We'll just keep it up until the feeding frenzy moves on," Karlie added reassuringly. She dabbed sunscreen onto her freckled nose.

"Good thing your parents aren't internet people."

"I know, right?"

But, in the elevator, guilt began to twist my stomach. The photo was out there forever. How was I going to keep this secret?

Through the hotel doors, the beige sands and gentle crush of late afternoon waves waited, and the tart ocean air was already making me thirsty. I took a big slurp from my water bottle and popped a piece of saltwater taffy.

We walked along the boardwalk, stepped onto the sand, and slipped off our flip-flops, carrying them to the first open spot we could find on the crowded beach. My uncles set up a big, blue umbrella. While my aunts checked the younger kids for adequate sunscreen, we checked our apps for likes, retweets, and shares.

"Up to eighty-six thousand on Insta." Chelsea groaned.

"Still trending on Twitter," Karlie muttered.

"And plenty of haters, I see." I scrolled through the top tweets. They were calling me "Crazy Eyes." And those were the *nice* ones. What was wrong with people?

"Let's take another selfie," Chelsea said quickly.

I sighed, but we clustered together and threw on smiles with our backs to the boardwalk.

"Cute," Chelsea said. "You can even see the Dolles sign in the background. Now I'll just pick a filter and—"

"Again with the phones?" Aunt Marilyn held out a hand. "Chelsea, that's enough. You girls are going to get tendonitis."

Chelsea immediately clicked to post the photo—#nofilter—and handed over her phone.

"Are you putting a photo on the internet?" Aunt Marg asked, looking peeved behind her oversized sunglasses. She was the oldest of the sisters, as well as the least amused by the rest of the world. If Mom was a digital dinosaur, Aunt Marg was a digital . . . whatever came before dinosaurs. I could Google that later.

"It's not safe to post photos on the internet," she continued. "Of yourselves in bikinis, no less. What if a predator sees it?"

"It's just our faces and the Dolles sign, Aunt Marg," Karlie said.

"So the predator will know where to find you, then."

"Don't scare the kids," Mom said, unfolding a beach chair. "But seriously, girls. Let's have a phone break for the next hour. This is a vacation!"

We settled onto our towels. Aunt Marilyn and Uncle Tim started building a sand castle with the little kids. Aunt Marg marched her twins down to the water to practice their aquatic survival techniques.

"Oh, this is the *life*," Mom said, leaning back in her chair and digging her feet into the sand. On either side of me, Karlie and Chelsea sighed in agreement. I closed my eyes.

The cries of the seagulls and the rhythm of the waves were calming, and the sun warmed my skin. Maybe it was all going to blow over. I mean, how many photos went mini-viral every day on the internet? How many click-bait links had I followed this week alone: "Watch this baby panda eat a carrot!" "This gymnast's fail will BLOW YOUR MIND!" "35 Text Conversations That Got Real Awkward Real Quick."

I blew out a deep breath. "Want to swim?" I asked my cousins.

"Sure," Karlie said, sitting up with a luxurious stretch.

Chelsea shook her head. "This feels too good. Have fun."

Karlie and I trotted down to the water's edge.

"Now, everyone talks about the undertow, but you really want to worry about the rip current—they're *not* the same thing," Aunt Marg was telling another mom as we passed her.

"Good thing she doesn't like the internet," I said. "Can you imagine her in a comments section?"

Karlie giggled. "She would seriously be the queen of flame wars."

"Yeah," I agreed, but my eyes drifted. All the people on this beach. . . . How many of them were on Instagram?

"Hey." She grabbed my arm. "Don't worry. We're going to have a fun week, okay? And nobody's going to recognize you in the water." I nodded and managed a smile. Then I followed her into the surf. After an hour, Mom waved to us from the umbrella and we paddled in. Time to shower off. Each year, the first dinner of family week was with everybody at the closest pizzeria. The last night would be Aunt Sophia's birthday dinner.

We kept our hands off our phones until we got back to the room.

"Hey, our last selfie got a ton of likes," Chelsea announced.

"Uh-oh," Karlie muttered.

"What?" I demanded.

"Um . . . you know *The Midnight Show*, the one that does hashtag challenges on Twitter?"

My heart skipped a beat. "Yeah . . ."

"Well, someone retweeted the photo from the beach, and—"

Chelsea and I looked over Karlie's shoulders to read the post.

"Crazy Eyes from #WhenTheBrittMeetsTheFan is @RehobothBeach! First to post a selfie w/ her (w/ consent, dudes) wins today's #WebPicChallenge!"

Behind our posed grins, the Dolles sign photo-bombed. It might as well have been a bull's-eye.

I dropped onto the bed. My hair dripped on my knees as the room spun around me.

"Is this even legal?" Karlie asked.

"Unbelievable." Chelsea shook her head. "So it's like a scavenger hunt? Or capture-the-flag?"

"Yeah," I said. "And I'm the flag."

* * * * *

"Are you sure you're okay?" Mom asked again.

I nodded. "Fine." Sweat beaded on my neck, but I wasn't taking this hoodie off.

The whole family—a giant, twenty-person amoeba—headed into the pizzeria at the north end of the boardwalk. It took literally two minutes to walk from our hotel, but the early evening air was so heavy and hot that I was already dying in my incognito sweatshirt.

I stuck to the center of the family amoeba with Karlie and Chelsea. They had been in the selfie, too, so we were all wearing sunglasses. I'd just have to be back to our room before twilight, when there would be no excuse to wear them. Missing the first night on the boardwalk would be awful, but it just seemed too risky.

Aunt Marg had called ahead to make sure there would be enough tables. There were so many of us that we took up half the restaurant. Thank goodness there was air conditioning. We staked out our seats and breathed in the savory air. Hands grabbed my shoulders, and I flinched hard.

It was only Dad. "Just wanted to get the tension out of those shoulders. What's up?"

"Poor Peanut must not be feeling well," Grandpa answered as he claimed the last chair at our table. "Don't worry, I'll brave the germs and sit next to her." He winked at me.

We all took our seats. I cringed as Britt Allen's newest single pounded through the speakers. It had sounded so much better two nights ago.

As soon as everyone had drinks, Grandpa stood up, raising his cup. "I want to officially welcome everybody to family week—from our newest grandbaby, Lewis, all the way up to the almost-birthday girl, my *older* sister, Sophia."

"More mature, at least," Aunt Sophia retorted, crossing her thin arms with a smirk. Everyone laughed.

"All right, all right," Grandpa said, raising a hand. "It's true." He glanced down at us with a smile. "I guess Delia kept me young all those years. But remember, it all started here—"

"Summer of '64," Mom and my aunts said in unison, clinking their glasses.

"Back then, you could get a whole pizza for under two dollars!" Grandpa gently tapped our server on the shoulder. "Any chance you would honor that price tonight, miss? I'm buying, see."

She chuckled and shook her head.

He shrugged with a grin. "Worth a shot. Anyways, let's all raise our glasses. To family, summer, and a terrific week together."

"Hear, hear," everyone chorused.

I shrank in my seat and fiddled with the toggles on my sweatshirt, hoping that we weren't drawing the eyes of anyone who watched *The Midnight Show*. Which was worse at this point: being grounded on vacation or being paparazzied by a stranger?

By the time our pizzas were served—topped with the signature swirls of pepperoni and cheese I looked forward to each year—my stomach was in knots.

"Hey," said Dad. "Look what I picked up in the gift shop, guys."

He held up a selfie stick. "Think we can fit everyone into a shot before we eat?"

Please, no.

Everybody chimed in their approval, except for Chelsea and Karlie. Dad quickly came over to me.

"Okay, Leigh, can you show—"

"No!" I exploded out of my seat. "No selfies!"

There was no way this was going to work. I had a room key in my pocket and I was using it. This was miserable. "I'm not feeling well," I mumbled.

Ignoring the concerned voices, I reached the boardwalk. I stumbled on, even as tears fogged up my sunglasses.

"Wait up, Peanut!"

I hesitated. Should I keep going?

"I know you can outrun an old man," Grandpa added. "But we *could* sit down and talk about what's going on."

I wiped my eyes. I didn't want to ruin Grandpa's first night, too. I turned around.

He was already settling onto the closest bench. "Good thing you didn't run," he said. "I really didn't have a backup plan."

I managed a grim smile and sat next to him, dropping my sunglasses in my lap. Maybe I could at least come clean to someone who wouldn't have any idea what I was talking about.

"Grandpa, I messed up." I took a deep breath. "The other night, I snuck out to a Britt Allen concert with Jenna when we were supposed to be studying for finals. One of the roadies got us backstage, but a photo I took with Britt went viral—um, that means thousands of people saw it and reposted it online, even though I didn't want them to, and—"

Grandpa held up a hand. "I know, Leigh."

I sat straight up. "How?"

He shrugged. "I follow you on Instagram."

My jaw dropped. He *followed* me? Grandpa—who yelled at remote controls and called GPS "just a lazy map"—*he* was on Instagram?

"Wait. Your phone was out when you had that coughing fit in the car. Was that why?"

His shoulders shook with a gentle chuckle. "You girls spent all afternoon trying to bury that photo in your feeds, and all you got for it was that moron from *The Midnight Show* inviting fanboys to stalk you. Peanut, this is a fine mess."

I couldn't find any words. I just leaned against him and nodded.

Grandpa sighed. "This boardwalk was simpler when I met your grandma," he said. "Simple, but so exciting! It was the summer after I graduated high school, and I was just a year older than you are now. I sold dime tickets at Funland and kept the Skee-Ball machines running. Delia was selling taffy and chocolates over at Dolles. The night our friends fixed us up. . . ." He chuckled again. "Well, we didn't need apps or emojis. I still had grease on my hands from a cranky Skee-Ball machine and cracked a joke about it being 'a hard day's night'—because that song had just topped the charts—and Dee's eyes lit up like the moon. When we got married, we agreed we'd bring the family here every year. A good way to keep us all grounded, remind us where we started.

"None of which applies to your situation, I realize," he added, "except—"

He pulled out his cellphone. "I believe the challenge was to be the 'first' person to post a selfie with you, right? Once someone does, the challenge is over?"

I broke into a smile. Of *course*.

Grandpa held out his phone, muttering under his breath while he put it in "selfie" mode. He snapped a photo and showed it to me.

"Maybe this will help you remember where you started."

I leaned over his arm, watching in wonder while he tweeted it out, hashtags and all. "Grandpa, how can I thank you?"

He looked at me. "By coming clean to your parents. You'll feel better once you do."

I nodded slowly. He was right.

"And by giving up that confounded phone of yours for the week."

"But—"

Grandpa's eyes were serious. "I went seven decades with no smartphone—I think you can handle seven days. Quit checking your likes and shares, Peanut. Have a vacation."

A week without my phone was going to be tough.

But as I handed it over, I felt better already.

* * * * *

The colorful granny-square blanket looked just right on Aunt Sophia's shoulders. She had draped it over herself proudly, despite the heat. "I love my birthday gift," she declared.

"Happy Birthday, Auntie," Mom said, bending to give her a peck on the cheek. Then she slipped her arm around me. "Your squares look great."

I smiled. Crocheting was actually kind of fun. Karlie had asked us to make a blanket for her dorm room next.

"Also, happy end-of-the-week, love." She handed me my phone.

It felt heavy in my hand. I wasn't "happy" about the end of family week. After the initial confession to Mom and Dad, including my painful explanation of "going viral," things had turned out way better than I'd expected.

I mean, I was grounded, obviously—until the Fourth of July—but Grandpa had lobbied them for mercy, too. We had all agreed that being dubbed "Crazy Eyes" by hordes of internet trolls was a pretty effective punishment on its own.

There were no photos from the previous week in my phone—the giant ice cream cones we devoured two nights ago, Karlie freaking out over a horseshoe crab, my epic Skee-Ball battle with Grandpa—no photos, no selfies, no filters. No technology to store my memories.

And I'd remember everything just fine.

Grandpa sidled up to me with a plate of birthday cake in his hands. "I just sent you a link to an article, Peanut. You should check it out."

"Now?"

He nodded. I pulled up his text message. Chelsea and Karlie appeared behind him, craning for a view as I clicked the link.

"You went viral again," Chelsea said.

The headline on the *Buzzfeed* article read: "You Won't Believe the

Amazing Reason Behind This Grandpa's Selfie!"

My face split into a grin. "Holy cow, it's us."

"It got more likes than the original photo," Karlie added. "Isn't it awesome?"

I looked up at Grandpa. "Awesome," I echoed.

His eyes looked full over his warm smile. The rest of the world might see it as just another viral story. But to me, it was a reminder of where we started.

JOY GIVENS RESIDES IN PITTSBURGH, PENNSYLVANIA, WITH HER FANTASTIC HUSBAND, THEIR TWO REMARKABLE SONS, AND AN IMPOSSIBLY LOVABLE DOG. IN ADDITION TO HER WRITING, JOY IS THE OWNER AND LEAD TUTOR OF GIVENS ACADEMIC AND PREPARATORY TUTORING, A COMPANY SERVING THE GREATER PITTSBURGH AREA. JOY'S PREVIOUSLY PUBLISHED WORKS INCLUDE THE YOUNG ADULT NOVEL *UGLY STICK*, THE SHORT STORY COLLECTION *APRIL'S ROOTS*, AND THE NONFICTION GUIDE *THE NEW SAT HANDBOOK*. JOY HAS FOND MEMORIES OF VISITING REHOBOTH BEACH AS A CHILD WITH HER FAMILY, AND SHE IS LOOKING FORWARD TO KEEPING UP THE TRADITION WITH A WHOLE NEW GENERATION!

The Understudy

By Terri Kiral

A welcomed quiet hovered softly over the early morning streets of Manhattan's Upper West Side. I started the ignition and exhaled along with the lethargic stutter of the engine. A dry puff of smoke blew from the muffler of my twelve-year-old Toyota, as if the release of toxins propelled it in motion. Finding my empty green eyes in the rearview mirror, I whispered tenderly, "It will get better. I promise." Leaving this early on a Tuesday would help me avoid the worst of the traffic. Estimated drive time was just under four hours. I'd get there well before noon.

My directional compass when driving seemed to often be missing its needle, and I hated it when people used words like "west" when I asked for directions. But I arrived at the bungalow with no wrong turns. I took the six, gray, sun-faded, wooden stairs of the front porch, two at a time. Tiny Indian brass bells, strung alternately with colored beads on an emerald cord, hung from the doorknob. They jingled hello when I walked in.

I opened a window to freshen the stale inside air. The ocean breeze from a block away promised to deposit a fine dust of therapeutic sea salt crystals on the furniture surfaces. A teal door off to the side of the kitchen opened to a secluded cedar deck that had been transformed into a meditation nook. An amber-colored resin statue of Buddha in Lotus Pose rested in the corner. Pointy, jagged-edged seashells, mingled with smooth beach glass, laid a natural carpet at his feet. *Balance.* Yellow butterflies, with papery, translucent wings, played among the white flowers of the perennial wild comfrey plants.

The glossy, heart-shaped leaves of the Canadian wild ginger ground cover introduced stark contrast. I picked a stem of foliage from the sweet goldenrod—Delaware's state herb—and crushed it between my fingers to release the distinctive scent of anise Tara had told me about. An incense burner sat on a round rattan table next to a weather-worn rocking chair, whose faded gray wood matched the front porch steps. *More balance.* Thanks to Tara, my roommate, who inherited this bungalow in Rehoboth Beach from her aunt, I had the opportunity to get out of New York City, away from my grueling job as general manager at Dagwood's Restaurant. Rent-free. Ten days.

The full-sized kitchen was a treat compared to the constraints of a two-burner stove and dorm-sized fridge in our Manhattan studio apartment. I was eager to try out some new vegetarian recipes I picked up at the studio where Tara taught yoga. The local farmers market was known for its ample selection of fresh produce. It opened in an hour, giving me enough time to freshen up.

Shy, early morning sunlight shimmered through the sheer, violet bathroom curtains. I unpacked my toiletries and found the guest towels in a cylindrical wicker basket in the corner. I looked forward to an energizing shower. The cool scent of organic mint shampoo cleansed both my dirty-blonde hair and my lungs. The herbal essence of Clary sage soap lifted my dreary spirits.

As I left the bungalow, the lingering hint of mint, mixed with the play of the sun's rays, shrouded me in an aromatic halo. I stopped at the bottom of the front porch steps and rocked up on sneakered tiptoes. Tilting my head back to greet the sun, both hands holding the cross-strap of my purse, I breathed in. The soft, repetitive roar from the ocean waves nearby made me anticipate meditating on the beach.

White tents with peaked roofs were arranged in orderly rows at the farmers market. Bright- colored berries, melons, and vegetables made me appreciate my healthy eating habits. Homemade jams, local honey, and unique artisan crafts convinced shoppers they were in need. A grunge-clad, grubby-faced acoustic guitarist sat under a tent, crooning tenderly to the market-goers, a James Taylor-like seduction in his voice. My heart sank as my thoughts turned immediately to Todd.

Being a solo music act, Todd was also his own agent, driver, and roadie. He had been doing back-to-back gigs in the city for months without a break, and it was wearing him down. At least that's what I thought at the time. In our ten years together, he never once raised his voice to me. I was confused by his recent callous manner and biting words. I carefully asked questions, trying to find an underlying issue causing his peculiar behavior. When my curiosity crept too close, he withdrew. Todd always had a lack of strength when it came to emotional confrontation. I knew enough to back off.

Effortlessly joining the secret society of unhappy couples, I had succumbed to participating in the charade of a healthy bond. The weight of unbalanced energy faltered around us like the low rumbling of an approaching avalanche. It threatened collapse while constantly watching from the back stage of our relationship. I stepped delicately through each day, cautious not to challenge gravity and trigger the snowslide. It exhausted me.

"I'm thinking of this skirt with the black top. You know, the one with the shoulders cut out," I said, holding the black-and-white tulle, tiered miniskirt over my forearm and presenting it to Todd. With New Year's Eve just six days away, I had wanted to get my outfit together for his gig.

He stood next to the towering wood cabinet we had built together for our Greenwich Village studio apartment. The one small closet wasn't nearly enough for both our clothes. The cabinet fit my clothing plus some of Todd's things. With eyes cast down, Todd quietly said, "You're not going."

After a three-second pause that held crushing heaviness for eternity in its minuscule space, I whispered, "What?" My eyes searched for his hidden ones while both the speed and volume of my heart increased. To be honest, I had known this moment was coming. No amount of tiptoeing around his extreme sensitivity to emotion could avoid the inevitable.

"You're not going," he repeated a little more sternly, offering nothing more, his gaze still lowered in unmistakable cowardice.

"What do you mean I'm not going?" I asked in disbelief. "I always go with you on New Year's Eve, every year for the last ten years." I tried to swallow the lump in my throat.

Todd gave no response. His silent, cold shoulder was delivered with the precision of razor-sharp edges on a gigantic iceberg slicing through the hard, gray metal side of a ship, sinking it into icy waters. I unconsciously shivered and placed a hand on the invisible gash in my gut. I asked anyway, "Is someone else going with you?"

"Yes."

That "yes" was the first of many concrete blocks to come. I gradually erected an impenetrable, award-winning wall, the likes of which no architect could possibly duplicate.

After Todd and I split, I got by well enough, but things were tight. With no one to share expenses, there was little left for any extras in life. I found a smaller apartment on the Upper West Side. Tara, my yoga teacher, came along at the right time. She shared a studio apartment with three others and was looking for more space. We had a lot in common and turned out to be perfect roommates. She was good medicine for me.

"Get out there. Meet some people. Go on a date, will ya?" Tara would say.

Her consistent urging was responsible for my only two dates in the last five years. Both were disasters. The first guy got out his selfie stick in the middle of dinner to take a picture of him and his food.

He said he wanted his ex-wife to see how well he was doing without her. Then came Patrick. He had upbeat energy and a dazzling, white smile. When discussing the latest books I purchased, he sat up straight and said, "I never read. I wait for the movie. It's always better." After that, I gave up on the dating game and launched myself full force into my job at the restaurant.

"You're beginning to permanently smell like a fryer," Tara had told me one day, wrinkling her nose. "And weren't you just complaining about finding a chin hair when you woke up a few days ago? Most men don't take to women with excessive facial hair. Better get busy before a full beard comes in," she joked. I rolled my eyes and chuckled to go along with the humor. I knew it was time to get back out there, but I wanted the connection to happen organically.

The buttery aroma of fresh-roasted garlic curled through the air, whetting appetites. The central tent of the farmers market was set up for cooking demonstrations. The chef, in white smock and checkered pants, looked intently at me. My initial thought was, *What are you looking at, buddy?* I jerked my head away, pretending not to notice, and continued to walk by.

The next tent was selling fresh flowers. I reached for a bouquet of daisies and felt a provocative warmth on my bare shoulders. Looking up, I noticed the sun hiding behind slow-moving clouds. I glanced behind me. The chef's eyes met mine, again. This time, I sent my own penetrating gaze. My raised eyebrows, wide-opened eyes, and tight slit for a mouth extinguished any possibility of welcome. I raised the daisies to cover my face, another layer of protection. Peeking between the petals, I watched the chef's smile wilt as he looked away.

While putting away the veggies I purchased at the farmers market, the neon-green sticky note resting on the middle shelf in the fridge begged attention. *Open your heart. Let someone in today.* I recognized Tara's handwriting, the large, rounded letters revealing her outgoing personality and artistic talent. A flood of Todd memories washed over me. It was five years ago, on a New Year's Eve, when my Titanic went down.

For some reason, the message in Tara's note captured me like a life preserver rescuing a drowning victim. I remembered the vow I made to myself at the start of this trip. "It will get better. I promise." My thoughts drifted to the chef at the market. I had been unkind. He hadn't deserved the ugly, icy glare I used to freeze-dry his ego. Ever since Todd dumped me, I was pushing people away, and I knew it. People had their hearts broken every day, but my brokenness spread as the years passed, like the branches of an untended crack in a windshield.

Last month, Tara spent hours secretly searching for Todd on social media. She wasn't good at deception, so I was onto her the entire time. I didn't say anything, though. I knew she meant well. She was looking to find one morsel of something—anything—to ease my suffering. And then, one night, just as the page appeared on the laptop, I stepped behind her.

"What are you looking at?"

We both stared in silence. Even the background soundtrack of perpetual New York City traffic dispersed into the ether.

"Can you believe it? It's uncanny," Tara said.

"LOVE MY WIFE. SHE'S ONE IN A MILLION," read the caption under the photo.

Shoulder-length, dirty-blonde hair, big green eyes, and a heart-shaped face mirrored my own. Even the square, marcasite ring on his wife's wedding finger matched the one Todd had given me on our second Christmas together.

"I heard he dated her years ago, but I had no idea she looked so much like me." My eyes didn't blink, never left the screen.

"You could be twins," Tara remarked.

At first, I felt flattered—triumphant even—that he picked someone who looked so much like me. But then, feeling the fool, I realized it was the other way around. Todd picked me because I looked like her. What did that mean for all those years we shared? Was I merely a look-alike substitute while he patiently waited for his real love? Was I just the understudy, conveniently tucked away temporarily in the wings, while he anticipated the stage entrance of his true shining star? Oh God. My downcast eyes could almost see my freshly crushed heart. It was as if the breakup happened just moments ago. He never loved me. It was her, all those years. Not me. He selfishly stole ten years of my life to temporarily fill his void. Hurt and anger took up permanent residence in my heart. Any precious memories I once cherished were corrupt, leaving a trail of viral destruction in their wake.

I put the daisies in a large mason jar standing by the kitchen sink, grabbed my yoga bag, and headed to the beach. Todd and I once spent a weekend here together, and it was difficult not to think of him. Passing by the candy store, my thoughts took me back to that time. I still had a picture of us sharing a five-foot piece of red licorice on the boardwalk, one end in each of our mouths, leaving those passing by to imagine what would happen when the ends met. That's the last time I ate red licorice.

This perfect summer afternoon hosted blue skies, soft sun, and a comfortable seventy-seven-degree temperature. I spread my multi-colored Mexican serape in the sand and placed my purple yoga mat on top. Sitting cross-legged, I faced the ocean. With eyes closed, and my hands resting on my thighs, I welcomed the misty breeze and imagined it blowing away the crowded thoughts in my mind. I visualized a waterfall gently cascading down my torso and cleansing out negative residue from the past. *Breathe in, healing energy. Breathe out, negative energy.* With my face bravely exposed to the elements,

I released the festering pain I was no longer able to contain. Briny tears, combined with salty air, burned like rivers of lava flowing down my cheeks. I surrendered and let them flow in cadence to my silent mantra. *Let it go. Let it go. Let it go.*

The steady ebb and flow of the ocean waves paired with the rhythm of my breath. I leaned back on my elbows and stretched my long, lean legs out in front of me. The clean air, the music of seagulls, the hope that rested beyond the horizon—they swelled in my view, appearing to me like a distant mirage coming into focus.

I had missed so much for too long.

Tara's note was right. It was time. *Open your heart. Let someone in today.* I would no longer live in the land of Todd—of "what if" and "how dare he." A fresh courage and longing to passionately participate in life was reborn.

A stinging spray of sand suddenly slapped my tear-stained face, and the surprise returned my wandering thoughts to the moment. A shiny, red surfboard flipped the corner of my blanket. I watched its owner squat down to brush away the sand, and gave my eyes permission to take in the way his thigh muscles rippled up and down below his blue, hibiscus-patterned swim trunks when he bent his knees. The rolling topography of his toned chest didn't escape me, either. *It's him.*

Remembering me from the farmers market, he nervously said, "My blanket is just a few feet back. I spotted you when you got here and wanted to say hello. I didn't plan on such a clumsy greeting, though. Sorry about the sand." He drew back slightly, and I saw a shield, not unlike my own, ready to ricochet approaching icicles.

"No worries," I replied. I welcomed this opportunity for redemption and said, "Hey, I owe you an apology for the ice-queen performance this morning. You didn't deserve that. My bad memories. Not your fault. I'm sorry."

He nodded. It was a kind gesture that let me off the hook.

"Yoga, huh?" the chef said, using his dimpled chin to point at my mat.

"Ya, yoga." I smiled at him.

"Nice. I've been meaning to give that a try."

"Why don't you? You're missing out," I suggested.

"A little out of my comfort zone."

"Speaking of comfort zones," I said, looking at the surfboard, "that's way out of mine. I can't swim."

"Really? Now *you're* the one missing out. How about I teach you to swim and you teach me yoga?"

"Hmm. I don't know . . . I almost drowned when I was six. I haven't been in the water since."

"It's not that hard," he coaxed with a smile. "And that way, neither of us will be missing out."

Again, I thought of Tara's note. *Open your heart. Let someone in today.* "Well, I guess I really should know how to swim."

"Do you like candy?" he asked.

"Sure." I laughed, thinking it an odd question. "Who doesn't like candy?"

"I own the cafe with the attached candy store on the boardwalk. Will you meet me there at eight o'clock tonight? We can share our first pointers and then maybe take a walk on the beach."

"OK," I replied.

"Great," he said with a big grin. "See you later, yogi girl."

I smiled at the "yogi girl" and watched him walk away carrying his surfboard, steadied with ease, on his muscled shoulder. My gaze lingered.

"Hey," I called after him. "Do you sell red licorice at your candy store?"

He turned around. "Sure do. I've got five-foot ropes of the stuff," he answered.

"Save me a piece, will ya?"

I lay down to rest my head on the Mexican serape blanket. Releasing my breath, I welcomed the warm rays from the sun. Under the twinkling canopy of the night sky, the softly lit beach serving as my stage, I would be the shining star.

TERRI KIRAL IS THE AUTHOR OF "THE ABSENT FATHER," A SHORT STORY PUBLISHED IN *THE LIFE UNEXPECTED: AN ANTHOLOGY OF STORIES AND POEMS*. SHE ENJOYS SHARING MOMENTS OF HER LIFE THROUGH HER BLOG, WWW.WHIMSYWITHINBLOG.WORDPRESS.COM, HOPING THESE STORIES WILL CREATE OPPORTUNITIES FOR OTHERS TO EXAMINE AND EMBRACE THEIR OWN. TERRI'S WORK ALSO APPEARS ON VARIOUS GUEST BLOG POSTS. SHE CREDITS HER DAILY (ALMOST) MEDITATION PRACTICE WITH BREATHING LIFE INTO HER STORIES. IN ADDITION TO WRITING, SHE IS A CERTIFIED RYT200 YOGA TEACHER, OFFERING A SENSE OF CALM, FLEXIBILITY, AND BALANCE TO THE LIVES OF OTHERS. TERRI GREW UP IN A SMALL WESTERN PENNSYLVANIA COAL MINING TOWN AND HAS LIVED IN NINE STATES SINCE LEAVING HER ROOTS IN 1979. SHE HAS COME FULL CIRCLE TO RETURN TO A SMALL TOWN IN EASTERN PENNSYLVANIA WHERE SHE RESIDES WITH HER HUSBAND, ANDY, AND CAT, PYEWACKET. TERRI'S FIRST VISIT TO REHOBOTH BEACH WAS IN THE EARLY 1980S. SHE HAS BEEN RETURNING EVER SINCE.

Beach Life

2017 REHOBOTH BEACH READS JUDGES

Stephanie Fowler

Stephanie Fowler attended Washington College, a small liberal arts school in Chestertown that is renowned for its writing program. There she was awarded the Sophie Kerr Prize, the largest undergraduate literary award in the country. Fowler won the award for a collection of short stories based on her native roots on the Delmarva Peninsula. She was inspired to start Salt Water Media, a company designed to provide tools, products, and services for indie authors. The endeavor evolved from her love of writing and her own experiences with publishing her novel, *Crossings*.

Barbara Lockhart

Barbara Lockhart is a graduate of the MFA Program in Creative Writing at Vermont College. She received two Individual Artist Awards in Fiction from the Maryland State Arts Council for excerpts from her first novel, *Requiem for a Summer Cottage*, (SMU Press) and her short stories. She is also the recipient of a silver medal from the Indie Publishers Book Awards for her historical novel, *Elizabeth's Field*. Her most recent book, *The Night is Young*, won Finalist in the National Indie Excellence Book Awards. Lockhart is also the author of a textbook and nationwide program for the teaching of children's literature, *Read to me, talk with me*, and the author and co-author of four children's books, *Rambling Raft*, *Once a Pony Time*, *Mosey's Field*, and *Will's Tractor*. A native of New York City, Lockhart lives on the Eastern Shore of Maryland.

Laurel Marshfield

Laurel Marshfield is a professional writer, ghostwriter, developmental editor, and book coach who assists authors of nonfiction, fiction, memoir, and biography in preparing their book manuscripts for publication. She has helped more than 400 authors shape, develop, and refine their book manuscripts—by offering manuscript evaluation, developmental editing, book coaching, ghostwriting, and co-authorship—through her editorial services for authors business, Blue Horizon Communications, which is located in Rehoboth Beach, DE.

Mary Pauer

Mary Pauer received her MFA in creative writing in 2010 from Stonecoast, at the University of Southern Maine. Twice the recipient of literary fellowship awards from the Delaware Division of the Arts, Pauer publishes short fiction, essays, poetry, and prose locally, nationally, and internationally. She has published in *The Delmarva Review*, *Southern Women's Review*, and *Foxchase Review*, among others. Her work can also be read in anthologies featuring Delaware writers. She judges writing nationally, as well as locally, and works with individual clients as a developmental editor. Her latest collection, *Traveling Moons*, is a compilation of nature writing. Donations from sales help the Kent County SPCA equine rescue center.

William Peak

William Peak is the author of *The Oblate's Confession*, a work of historical fiction that took silver in the Best New Voice: Fiction category of the Benjamin Franklin Awards, won the National Indie Excellence Award for Religion: Fiction, and was awarded second place in the Catholic Novel of the Year category by the Catholic Press Association. *Kirkus Reviews* named *The Oblate's Confession* to its list of the best Indie books published in 2015. Peak's poetry and prose have been published in magazines and literary reviews. His poetry has been nominated for a Pushcart Prize. Peak received his undergraduate degree from Washington & Lee and his Master's from the creative writing program at Hollins University. When he's not writing fiction, Peak works for the Talbot County Free Library in Easton, Maryland, where he is regularly hailed on the streets of Easton: "Hey library guy!"

Judith Reveal

Judith Reveal is a freelance editor, book indexer, book reviewer, and author. She works with writers as an editor and coach and has edited nearly 100 manuscripts, many of which have gone on to publication. Reveal has taught creative writing classes at Chesapeake College as well as at arts councils across the Delmarva Peninsula. She presents workshops at the Bay to Ocean (BTO) Writers Conference, Harford County Library Writers Conference, Creative Writers Conference (Lewes, DE), and Dover Library. She has published short stories in local, regional, and national magazines and has five books published, including *The Four Elements of Fiction*. She is a book reviewer for the *New York Journal of Books* (www.nyjournalofbooks.com). Her website is www.justcreativewriting.com.

Want to see *your* story in a Rehoboth Beach Reads book?

The Rehoboth Beach Reads Short Story Contest

The goal of the Rehoboth Beach Reads Short Story Contest is to showcase high-quality writing while creating a great book for summer reading. The contest seeks the kinds of short, engaging stories that help readers relax, escape, and enjoy their time at the beach.

Each story must incorporate the year's theme and have a strong connection to Rehoboth Beach (writers do not have to live in Rehoboth). The contest opens March 1 of each year and closes July 1. The cost is $10/entry. Cash prizes are awarded for the top stories and 20–25 stories are selected by the judges to be published in that year's book. Contest guidelines and entry information is available at: *catandmousepress.com/contest.*

Also from Cat & Mouse Press

Other Rehoboth Beach Reads Books

The Sea Sprite Inn

Jillian has lived through more than her share of tough times, but leaps at a chance to reinvent herself when she inherits the responsibility for a dilapidated family beach house.

Sandy Shorts

Bad men + bad dogs + bad luck = great beach reads. The characters in these stories ride the ferry, barhop in Dewey, stroll through Bethany, and run wild in Rehoboth.

Children's Books

Fun with Dick and James

Follow the escapades of Dick and James (and their basset hound, Otis) as they navigate the shifting sands of Rehoboth Beach, facing one crazy conundrum after another.

How To Write Winning Short Stories

A concise guide to writing short stories that includes preparation, theme and premise, title, characters, dialogue, setting, and more.

Online Newspaper

Jam-packed with articles on the craft of writing, editing, self-publishing, marketing, and submitting. Free. Writingisashorething.com

Come play with us!

www.catandmousepress.com
www.facebook.com/catandmousepress

Cat & Mouse Press™

A Playful Publisher

CPSIA information can be obtained
at www.ICGtesting.com
Printed in the USA
LVHW02s1504141117
556257LV00011B/683/P